The Armageddon Syndrome

J. R. Church

All Scripture quotations are from the King James Version of the Holy Bible unless otherwise indicated.

BEACON STREET PRESS
500 Beacon Drive
Oklahoma City, OK 73127
1-800-652-1144
www.swrc.com

Printed in the United States of America

ISBN 978-1-933641-68-3

The Armageddon Syndrome

J. R. Church

Contents

Introduction

World leaders are infected by a cloud of political gloom spreading over our planet—prompting a former president of the United States to suggest that we may indeed live in that generation which will see the awesome Armageddon.

Concerted efforts are being made to bring warring factions to the peace table, but little hope is expressed.

The late Dag Hammarskjold, while serving as secretary general of the United Nations, sat at his desk, put his head in his hands, and wept, "We have tried so hard and failed so miserably!"

What does the future hold? Is there no hope at all? This book sheds light on the darkening political maze facing our world in the near future and reveals the electrifying remedy prescribed.

Foreword

J. R. Church was one of my heroes in the ministry. Growing up, I remember watching him each week on "Prophecy in the News." I also remember the excitement I felt when the *Prophecy in the News* magazine arrived each month in my mailbox. As a Christian broadcaster and publisher, J. R. Church was a man ahead of his time.

J. R. was born in 1938 in Abilene, Texas. He was named Jerry Rolan Church, but he was always known as J. R. He became a Christian at the age of seven in a home Bible study. Not long after God called him to ministry and J. R. set out with a goal in life to win others to Jesus Christ. It was reported that he won his first person to the Lord when he was only eight years old.

J. R. graduated from Lubbock High School in 1957, and he moved to Tennessee where he studied Bible at Tennessee Temple University. He ultimately was awarded a B.A. and later was granted an honorary Doctor of Divinity degree from Immanuel Baptist Theological Seminary in Peachtree, Georgia.

In 1958, J. R. Church married Linda and they had two children,a daughter, Terri, and a son, Jerry. J. R. served as the pastor of Western Hills Baptist Church in Lubbock, Texas, for seventeen years. He had a skill for teaching Bible prophecy and felt God moving him to start a ministry devoted to Bible prophecy. So, in 1979, J. R. Church moved to Oklahoma City and started "Prophecy in the News."

"Prophecy in the News" went on to become the premier television program dealing with current events in Bible prophecy. Consequently, J. R. became known as a respected Bible prophecy teacher. He was a frequent speaker at conferences and churches across the United States.

I was fortunate enough to have met J. R. Church a couple of times. One of those times was at a conference in 2003. I treasure the experience. J. R. signed a book for me and said, "Young man, just keep preaching Jesus and keep looking up."

J. R. went to be with the Lord in 2011, but his legacy continues through his writings and recordings. The book that you hold in your hand is proof of his continuing legacy. *The Armageddon Syndrome* was originally published in 1985. When I read through the original edition, I was amazed at how current and relevant the material was for today. So, I was very excited when Beacon Street Press agreed to bring *The Armageddon Syndrome* back for a new generation of readers.

This new edition of *The Armageddon Syndrome* has been revised and updated to include some of J. R.'s teachings on the High Holy Days. I think this book is one you will want to read and read again. I know that you will be blessed from the prophetic perspectives of J. R. Church. After reading this book, you will find yourself looking forward to the future Rapture of the saints. Until then, "Keep looking up."

—James Collins, Staff Evangelist
Southwest Radio Ministries

Part 1

What Does the Future Hold?

Chapter 1

Setting the Stage

During the twentieth century, Jews have been accused of controlling all money, causing all depressions, creating inflation, and plotting the conquest of the world. Some people think the Jews own everything. There seems to be nothing new under the sun. Jew accusers today are simply following the lead of the anti-Semitics before them. People who do not wish to accept responsibility for the wrongs in society must have a scapegoat. The Jewish people have been made a universal whipping boy. They take the blame for all kinds of problems—ranging from plagues to politics.

Even the bubonic plague that swept medieval Europe was blamed on the Jews. They were accused of having poisoned the water wells with a powder made of spiders, frog legs, Christian entrails, and communion bread. The public wrath that resulted from that fantastic tale brought about the slaughter of thousands of Jews and the complete extermination of two hundred Jewish communities.

This fierce hatred of Jews and the willingness to believe such outlandish accusations against them can only be explained as a fulfillment of Moses' prophecy in Deuteronomy 28:37: "And thou shalt become an astonishment, a proverb, and a byword, among all nations whither the Lord shall lead thee."

Poland became the next inviting oasis in the desert of Jewish persecution and dispersion. After being attacked and slaughtered in the beloved Rhine Valley by the Crusaders, many Jews fled to Poland.

The Jews who settled in Poland seemed to have found a stable sanctuary. There they were able to practice their Hebrew customs and were even allowed to use their own languages, Hebrew for religious purposes and Yiddish for secular life. They were granted partial political autonomy under the Polish crown and were governed by their own supreme council. Legal problems between Jews were settled by their own rabbinical courts, rather than by Polish law. Bible prophecies of suffering and persecution appeared to have overlooked the nearly ideal conditions the Jews were experiencing on Poland

They began to relax and feel safe. The persecutions of the past were far removed from them. Their lives were no longer in jeopardy as they began to prosper. They prospered financially, but the prophet's words were not to be denied.

The eighteenth century saw most of eastern Poland become part of the Russian Empire, and the quality of life for the Jews began to decline. Their autonomy was eroded. Once again came unwarranted domination. They were hounded and persecuted by czarist authorities and were confined to areas consisting mainly of small towns along the Russian and Polish borders.

Violent pogroms and oppression of Jews was rampant in Czarist Russia during the 19th and early 20th centuries.

In the latter part of the nineteenth century under Czar Alexander III, the persecution became almost unbearable. It was then that a new word entered the vocabulary of the Jews and Russians—the word *pogrom*. This term was adopted by Czar Alexander as a name for the organized massacres of the Jews carried out by soldiers who burned and murdered their way through Jewish settlements in western Russia.

Moses' warning that they would never find a place of ease must have come to mind as this battered people prepared for another exodus—this time from Russia.

Fleeing westward, many Jews arrived in the United Kingdom and in the United States. Seventy-five percent of the Jews in the United Kingdom and in the United States are of Russian descent.

Nazi "Yellow Star"

Social and economic sanctions were brought against the Jews in nearly every nation. Many countries barred Jews from owning land. They were not allowed to join craft guilds. At one time they were expelled from both England and France, and all their property was confiscated. The church forbade Jews to employ Christians and forbade Christians to live among Jews. The fourth Lateran Council of 1215 demanded that all Jews wear a distinguishing badge. In England, the Jews wore a replica of the tablets of the Ten Commandments; France and Germany demanded a yellow "O" similar to the yellow stars used by the Nazis of Hitler's Germany.

In Germany, Jews were forbidden to ride in carriages and were forced to pay a toll whenever they entered a city. In Venice, the Jews were required to lie in a particular area; the word used to designate their forced boundaries is the one from which we get the word "ghetto." In Russia, Jews were drafted for military service at the age of twelve and had to serve for twenty-five years. They were also forced to pay special taxes on kosher meat and Sabbath candles. Jewish women living in large university centers were required to wear the mark of a prostitute. And even these miseries had been foretold long ago:

> Thou shalt beget sons and daughters, but thou shalt not enjoy them; for they shall go into captivity. All thy trees and fruit of thy

> land shall the locust consume. The stranger that is within thee shall get up above thee very high; and thou shalt come down very low. He shall lend to thee, and thou shalt not lend to him: he shall be the head, and thou shalt be the tail.
>
> —Deuteronomy 28:41–44

The magnitude of Jewish suffering is difficult to comprehend. You may hear of sanctions, slaughters, persecutions, and prejudices, but these are likely to simply move through your mind as historic facts without telling the whole story. The real account of the miseries of the Jews is one of feelings, frustrations, and fears. That is the human side of history. Who can measure the hurt of being stigmatized, ridiculed, set apart, and hated? Imagine the horror of being separated from your loved ones and sold as a slave. Think of living under constant threat of death as did the Jews during the Cossack Rebellion, when one hundred thousand of them died through torture and violence in less than a decade.

Feel the grief of Jewish families when fifteen hundred of their relatives were executed in York, England, in one day under the decree of King John. How ironic it is that New York City has become the city with the world's largest Jewish population. Even in America, Jews have been the subject of jokes and ridicule. Here, too, the children of Israel have endured cutting remarks and *de facto* segregation.

Now that Arab oil is necessary for Americans to continue their love affair with affluence and travel, one wonders how long this nation will officially stand on the side of the Jews. Perhaps the lust for black gold will end the Golden Age of American Jewry. Can it be that the United States is about to become another Spain or Rhine Valley or Poland? Jewish favor has always been fragile, and oil may grease the slide in America. If so, the land of the free will enter its darkest hour.

Since the rejection and crucifixion of their Messiah, the story of the Jews has been one of misery. For many, life itself has been a burden, a thing to wish away—as Moses put it in Deuteronomy 28:67: "In the morning thou shalt say, would God it were even! And at even thou shalt say, would God that it were morning!"

Those who have wronged the Jews have fared no better than those they have persecuted. History's graveyards are filled with kings and generals who thought they could mistreat the Jews and get away with it. Actually, Jew-hating is a depraved luxury no nation can afford.

In his book *The World's Collision,* Dr. Charles Pont put it very well. He said"

> Anti-Semites are not only the enemies of the Jews; they are their own enemies and the enemies of mankind. All, from Pharaoh to Hitler, have been horribly judged for having fashioned the sword against these people. Czarist Russia came to an inglorious end, as did Hitlerism and Fascism. Many of these Anti-Semitics either committed suicide or were slain. But what about the children of Israel? Like Old Man River they seemed to roll along in spite of it all.

Long ago Abraham, the father of the Jewish nation, was given an unusual promise by the Lord. It was a guarantee of blessing which provided a judgment upon all who would bring evil upon his descendants. Genesis 12:2–3 reads: "And I will make of thee a great nation, and I will bless thee, and make thy name great; and thou shalt be a blessing: And I will bless them that bless thee, and curse him that curseth thee: and in thee shall all families of the earth be blessed."

It was Frederick the Great who said, "No nation ever persecuted the Jew and prospered." His correct observation is proof, I think, of God's faithfulness in keeping His promise to Abraham. Nebuchadnezzar, Herod, Titus, the Russian czar, Hitler, and scores of others are witnesses to this truth. The Jews are here to stay.

But there is another dimension to the story. The dispersion of Jews will not last forever. Through the long and difficult years of their suffering, the words of their prophets have continued to remind this scattered people that they would ultimately return to their land and there prosper under the leadership of their Messiah. To some, the idea seemed far-fetched. But to others, this hope brought light in the darkest hours. Each Passover and each Yom Kippur the Jews would say to each other, "Next year in Jerusalem." Sometimes it had a hollow sound. Often those who spoke the words did not really believe them. Nevertheless, the promise of the prophets was passed on from one generation to another.

Finally, a few dared to do more than just dream. An infant movement began that in less than a century would transport hundreds of thousands of Jews back to the land of their fathers.

After decades of struggle and war, a nation would be born, and it would be the most significant event of this century. The organization of the Zionist movement in the 1890s that led to the birth of the nation of Israel in 1948 is the greatest fulfillment of the Bible prophecy in twenty centuries. Many believed it marked the beginning of the end-time generation. It set the stage for Armageddon and the return of Jesus Christ to establish His golden kingdom wherein He will rule over the world as the King of kings and Lords of lords.

Anti-Semitism did not end with the birth of the nation of Israel in 1948. Though the world was ashamed of the Holocaust created by Hitler in Nazi Germany, the world still has a tendency to blame the Jews for its problems. Anti-Semitism is still very much alive today. Of all the nations in the world today, only the United States stands on the side of Israel, and now, even Washington is wavering.

Though Israel had managed to make peace with Egypt, the rest of the Arab world still desires to push the Jew into the Mediterranean. Where will it all end? Armageddon.

Chapter 2

The Jews Return

Jewish people returning to the land of the fathers in 1948.

It has been said that a third of the Bible contains prophecy. It is my opinion, however, that far more than that can be said to contain prophetic truth. With so much prophecy to be found in the

Bible, it is important, I think, for every Christian to understand the chronology of end-time events.

If you have a basic understanding of the sequence of events, many heretofore difficult passages will become clear and lay themselves in their proper order. Sometimes the Scripture will not deal specifically with a prophetic truth but will add highlights of otherwise hidden meaning through prophetic implication.

There are at least three ways a person can study a passage of Scripture: primary interpretation, practical application, and prophetic implication. Once a Christian understands the chronology of events, the prophetic implication of Scripture will begin to become clear.

Many prophecies relate to events that occur simultaneously, and it is difficult to list them in chronological order. However, we shall try.

First of all, the key that unlocks the door to end-time Bible prophecy is found in Matthew 24:32–34:

> Now learn a parable of the fig tree; When his branch is yet tender, and putteth forth leaves, ye know that summer is nigh: So likewise ye, when ye shall see all these things, know that it is near, even at the doors. Verily I say unto you, This generation shall not pass, till all these things be fulfilled.

This may not be the first event in God's timetable, but it is certainly the most important. The nation of Israel is pictured as a fig tree, and according to the prophecy, when the fig tree comes to life again, it will mark the last generation. No end-time prophecies can be fulfilled without the return of the Jew to his land.

Since the regathering of Israel and the reestablishment of a national Jewish homeland is one of the most important fulfillments of Bible prophecy in this generation, many of the Old Testament prophets wrote of this event. Among them was Jeremiah, who gave an unusual description of Israel's unique return. "Turn, O Backsliding children, saith the Lord; for I am married unto you: and I will take you one of a city, and two of a family, and I will bring you to Zion" (Jeremiah 3:14).

Please note the detail "one of a city, and two of a family." This is exactly what happened in the late 1940s when the beleaguered Jewish people fled the ravages of Europe and Germany. Oftentimes, a Jewish immigrant would be heard to say something like this, "I am the only one in our family from Berlin who has survived. But I've just met one other member of the family who has also survived—my uncle from Hanover."

In each story the name of the town might differ; the country might be Poland or Austria rather than Germany. Instead of an uncle it might be a nephew or cousin or married sister. But the essential feature of Jeremiah's prophecy remains the same—"one of a city, and two of a family." Yes, the prophecy of Jeremiah has come to pass—even in the smallest detail. After 1,813 years of wandering among the nations of the world, suffering severely in every generation, a remnant has returned. The Jew is back in his land.

The modern Zionist movement is the culmination of many attempts down through the centuries to restore the nation of Israel.

In almost every century, attempts have been made to regather the people and restore the nation, but all have failed until, in the providence of God, the prophecy was to be fulfilled.

Through the centuries, however, the Jews managed to maintain their identity as a people. They kept their faith in the book of the Law, in the writings of the rabbis, and in the observance of the Sabbath.

One factor which helped to keep the desire for the Promised Land alive in the Jewish heart was the ever-present threat of persecution. They suffered the slavery of imperial Rome and the persecution of religious Rome. In the year 1290, the Jews were expelled from England. For three hundred years no Jews were allowed in the country. When Shakespeare wrote his play, "The Merchant of Venice," he painted a portrait of the Jewish people in the person of a character called Shylock. He projected a stereotype of a people who were thought to be treacherous and covetous, whose only profession was usury—such was the concept the English had of the Jews from the thirteenth to the sixteenth centuries.

It is said that the worst sufferings of the Jewish people were inflicted upon them by Christians. Christian anti-Semitism declared that the Jews were guilty of "deicide," the murder of God. Many believed that the Jews were under a perpetual and irrevocable curse of God.

False rumors followed the Jews wherever they went. It was generally believed that the Jews murdered Christian children to use their blood for secret ceremonies connected with the Passover. They were accused of everything from spreading plagues to plotting a world takeover. They were "Christ-killers" to be despised and tormented.

Under twenty centuries of severe persecution there was just one ray of light for dispersed Israel—Zion. It has been the dream of the Jew in every generation to return to Zion. From time to time, a leader would arise and attempt to lead an expedition back to the Promised Land. For instance, in the year 1525, David Reubeni appeared in western Europe and sought to raise an army to reconquer Palestine. He came from the east and announced that his brother was the ruler of a Jewish kingdom in the Middle East near the Promised Land. He even presented himself to the pope, and, amazingly enough, the pope received him, endorsed him, and sent him off with a letter of recommendation to the king of Portugal, Charles V, who was emperor of the Holy Roman Empire.

The Jewish people throughout Europe rallied to David Reubeni and felt that the time had finally come to return home again. Unfortunately, when Reubeni finally reached Charles V, he was arrested and executed. The resulting fifteenth century Inquisition in Spain and Portugal seemed to seal the fate of his brethren. Jews were forced to convert to Catholicism or die. In many cases, if the church was not satisfied that their conversion was genuine, they died anyway.

Toward the end of the fifteenth century (according to one pilgrim) the city of Jerusalem was almost devoid of inhabitants. Only four thousand families lived in Jerusalem. Of these, only seventy families were Jewish, and they were "of the poorest class, lacking even the commonest necessities." Such was the description of an early pilgrim on the plight of the Jews in Palestine. The desolation of the land had somehow come to stand for the miserable state of the Jewish people. Both were desolate; both were in hostile hands; both awaited God's redemption.

In the sixteenth century the Jews again experienced a brief moment of hope. Joseph Nasi, a wealthy Portuguese Jew who had fled to Turkey, rose high in the favor of the sultan. The title of Nasi, Duke of Naxos, was bestowed upon him. He was given an island in the Aegean Sea and was granted complete rights to the Tiberius section of northern Palestine.

Joseph Nasi planned to use his great wealth and influence to settle a large number of Jewish families around the Sea of Galilee. Silkworms, he decided, would provide the means of livelihood for his colony. Before the plan could be implemented, however, war broke out between Turkey and Venice. In the turmoil, Joseph Nasi fell from favor and lost his power. Again, Jewish hopes were dashed.

But with that failure in the sixteenth century there arose another ray of hope—this time coming from England. With the translation of the Bible into English in the 1500s, there developed a renewed confidence in the authority of the Scriptures. The Christians in England began to understand the prophecies of a restored Israel.

In 1589, Francis Kett expounded upon the theory of a regathered Israel. His ideas, however, cost him his life. He was declared a heretic and burned at the stake. But the dream did not die with him. Other Elizabethan churchmen, including the Puritans, began to speak and write about the predicted Jewish homeland—the restoration of Israel.

Most of those early theologians believed that the Jews would convert to Christianity, whereupon God would forgive them for their unbelief and restore them to their land. In 1621, Sir Henry Finch published a book entitled *The Restauration of Jews,* in which he wrote that "all the gentiles shall bring their glory into thy empire." Such a statement provoked immediate and violent opposition in both the church and the state.

King James I considered the book personal libel and arrested the elderly Sir Henry and his publishers. Though they were held only a few weeks, it had a chilling effect upon seventeenth century English theologians. Still, despite opposition and persecution, the idea had taken root and would continue to grow among the Puritans and others. Someday, they said, the Jews will re-establish the nation of Israel!

The Christian concept of a restored Jewish nation of Israel flourished in England between 1640 and 1666. It was believed that the regathering of the Jews to their homeland would usher in the messianic age and the millennium.

There was a flurry of ideas. Among them was the belief that the English were members of the ten lost tribes of Israel. This gave rise to the theory called "British Israelism." The English were Anglo-Saxons, and the word Saxon was thought to be a derivative of the term "Isaac's sons." The Danish people were conjectured to be descendants of the tribe of Dan, and the name of Denmark, some suggested, was a derivative of "Dan's mark."

Sabbatai Zevi

In the year 1666 a Jewish tradesman in Smyrna gained widespread attention when he proclaimed himself the Messiah of the Jewish people. His name was Sabbatai Zevi. He announced that in the year 1666 he would lead his people back to their homeland. Hopes revived. Some thought the time had come and that the Messiah had appeared.

When Zevi left Smyrna, in western Turkey and traveled to Constantinople in 1666, he found that he had taken on an impossible task. Instead of taking the sultan's crown, he became the prisoner of the Turkish ruler. It is said that he was given the choice of converting to Islam or dying, whereupon this self-proclaimed Messiah of the Jews promptly became a devotee of Mohammed. Once again Jewish hopes crumbled.

During the same period, two books were written by Christians who studied the biblical prophecies. The first book was entitled *Nova Solyma,* written by Samuel Gott and published anonymously in 1648. It was a utopian novel about the return of the Jews to their homeland. Gott was said to have been influenced by John Milton, author of *Paradise Lost.* The book disappeared, however, and only came to light again in 1902.

Another such book of the period was called *The Way of Light,* by Johann Amos Comenius, who foresaw a messianic age that would be preceded by the restoration of the Jews in their land. Its author was a Czechoslovakian living in England. His book was published in Latin in 1667. It, too, dropped out of sight and was rediscovered, translated into English, and printed in 1938. Both of these books, among others, were three hundred years ahead of their time in their espousal of the idea of a regathered Israel.

The Puritans in the early 1600s adopted the idea that the Indians in the New World must be the ten lost tribes of Israel. Many were the strange and unusual theories that arose in the wake of the Protestant Reformation and the translation of the Bible into English. Not all theories were based upon an accurate interpretation of the Bible.

The most significant Jewish leader in the 1600s was Manasseh ben Israel, rabbi of Amsterdam. His book, entitled *The Hope of Israel,* linked the messianism of the British Puritans with that of the Jews. The rabbi accepted the Puritan notion that the Indians of the New World made up the ten lost tribes of Israel.

His studies in the book of Daniel, coupled with the prophecy from Deuteronomy that the Jews would be scattered from one end of the earth to the other, convinced him that those Indians must be Jews. Furthermore, he believed that England must re-admit Jews within her borders, and he worked together with British Christians to bring this about.

While Manasseh ben Israel believed in the regathering of Israel, many of the Jews during the seventeenth and eighteenth centuries did not agree. The idea of a restored and regathered Israel was largely a Christian concept. It has been the evangelical Christian community over the past two hundred years who promoted the concept of a regathered Israel in their national homeland.

In 1787 Joseph Priestley, a world-renowned naturalist, philosopher, and theologian, proposed that Jews acknowledge Jesus as their Messiah, come to the end of their sufferings, and be regathered into the Holy Land.

Why, the very idea! Suggesting that the Jews acknowledge Jesus as the Messiah! Such a thought was disgusting to the Jews in 1787. In fact, David Levi, the first Jew to translate the Pentateuch into English, responded to Joseph Priestley with anger and revulsion. Most of the devout Jews of his day were not anticipating either the coming of the Messiah or a return to their land.

In 1799, Napoleon Bonaparte invaded Palestine and was called upon by the British Christian Restoration Movement to grant the Jews a homeland. They believed that the fall of the Turkish Ottoman Empire was inevitable and felt that the time had come for the regathering of Israel. Napoleon's victory was short-lived, however, and his retreat after only one month ended the immediate hope of restoration.

There were many people during the nineteenth century who embraced the concept of a restored Jewish State. They were men like John Adams, Robert Browning, and Benjamin Disraeli. One of the most colorful was Sir Laurence Oliphant, a member of the British parliament. In 1878, he set out to secure the land of Gilead east of the Jordan River for the Jewish people. In 1880, he went to Constantinople to see the sultan. It is said that the land of Gilead was bought from the Turkish government for the purpose of resettling the area with Jewish immigrants.

Though the land was bought and paid for by the Jews, the British occupied it in 1918. Three years later, in 1922, Winston Churchill, British secretary of the Colonies, partitioned the land of Palestine, created the Hashemite kingdom of Transjordan, and gave the land of Gilead to the Arabs. The Jews have never been allowed to possess Gilead, the territory they purchased. King Hussein of Jordan ruled over Gilead—refusing to recognize Jewish ownership of the land.

Sir Oliphant moved to Haifa in the 1880s in order to assist Jewish immigrants returning to their homeland. He died there in 1888.

New preparations for the return of Israel began in the late 1890s when Theodor Herzl organized the Zionist movement, an organization dedicated to the reestablishment of the nation of Israel.

Theodor Herzl

The name of Theodor Herzl is forever inscribed in history as "the father of modern Zionism." He conducted the first World Zionist Congress in Basel, Switzerland, in 1897, and declared afterward what appears to have been a prophetic statement: "At Basel I founded the Jewish State! If I said this out loud today, I would be greeted by universal laughter. In five years, perhaps, and certainly in fifty years, everyone will perceive it. ..."

Seven years later Theodor Herzl was dead, but exactly fifty years later, on November 29, 1947, the United Nations voted to establish a Jewish State in Palestine. Though it was not intended as a prophecy, the dream of Theodor Herzl came true.

Herzl was a Jew, but behind the scenes a Christian clergyman worked to bring Herzl's dream to reality. His name was William Hechler. He became convinced from his study of Bible prophecy that 1897 was the crucial year for the restoration of the Jewish State. When he read Theodor Herzl's book, *Der Judenstaat,* which translated means, "The Jewish State," Hechler went to Herzl and volunteered to help him bring the vision to reality.

Early in his career William Hechler had served as a tutor to the children of Frederick, Grand Duke of Baden, who was the uncle of Kaiser Wilhelm. He had showed them his biblical charts and diagrams, and he had persuaded the Grand Duke and other members of the German royal family that the Jewish State would be restored.

Furthermore, Hechler was British. Theodor Herzl knew that the British Christian community believed in the prophetic regathering of Israel and would probably be his strongest ally. He was right. Evangelical Christianity has always stood by the side of the Jewish people. Hechler arranged a two-hour audience for Herzl with Grand Duke Frederick, and in October of 1898 also arranged a meeting with Kaiser Wilhelm. They met both in Constantinople and in Jerusalem. The tireless efforts and prayers of William

Hechler on behalf of Theodor Herzl should not go unnoticed and should not be forgotten in history.

In 1902, the World Zionist Congress was offered the Sinai for settlement. The British had control of the land and offered to give it to the Jews. That plan collapsed, but in 1903 the African territory of Uganda was offered to the World Zionist Congress.

The British Foreign Office officially recognized the Zionist movement as a diplomatic entity in 1903 by their letter offering Uganda as a place of refuge for the Jews. Theodor Herzl was willing to accept the land in East Africa, but William Hechler, the Christian clergyman, argued that accepting Uganda would destroy all hopes of resettlement in their homeland of Palestine. By August 1904, Theodor Herzl was dead, and when the World Zionist Congress met again, it abandoned the Uganda plan.

Between 1904 and 1915 some forty thousand Jewish immigrants arrived in Palestine, nearly doubling the Jewish population.

The long winter of world history was coming to a close when General Allenby of the British army captured the city of Jerusalem in December of 1917 and took Megiddo by September of 1918, thereby carrying out Great Britain's Balfour Declaration, which stated, "His majesty's government views with favor the establishment in Palestine of a national homeland for the Jewish people. ..."

As the story goes, the British were suffering during World War I, having run out of gun powder and the raw materials with which to make explosives, The Germans had blocked the sea lanes in the Atlantic, and Britain could not get the necessary nitrates from their mines in Brazil. They brought the desperate situation to the

Two British Sergeants, Sedgewick and Hurcomb, who accepted the surrender of Jerusalem in 1917.

attention of a young scientist, Chaim Weizmann, who in a matter of two weeks developed a method by which the British could draw nitrogen from the air! Weizmann was credited with saving the British Empire in World War I. When asked what they could do to show their appreciation, Weizmann requested the land of Palestine as a homeland for his people, the Jews.

Allenby then was sent to Cairo to lead his regiment up through the desert, past Beersheba, to surround the city of Jerusalem on December 9, 1917. The night before his impending invasion, Allenby, being a Christian, prayed. He asked the Lord to let him take the city without destroying the holy places.

The next morning, he sent some British airplanes on a reconnaissance flight over the city. (Bear in mind that the Turkish occupiers of the city had never seen an airplane before. In 1917, British planes were odd looking contraptions!) That morning, while buzzing the Eastern Gate over the temple site, the British pilot dropped a note demanding surrender signed by General Allenby. Now, please understand that in the Arabic language *Allah* means God, and *beh* is a word for *son*. A Turkish soldier picked up a strange note dropped from a frightful "bird" demanding surrender, signed by Allah-beh, the son of God! When he took the note to his superior, a white flag was hoisted, and the city surrendered without firing a single shot—perhaps in fulfillment of Isaiah 31:5: "As birds flying, so will the Lord of hosts defend Jerusalem; defending also he will deliver it; and passing over he will preserve it."

The Balfour Declaration did not create a Jewish State, but it prepared the way for the events which led to the establishment of the nation of Israel in 1948. Please note: General Allenby was a Christian. William Hechler was a Christian. The British Restoration Movement was a Christian movement. Yes, over the past five hundred years, with the development of the printing press and the translation of the Bible into English, there came a return (in Protestant Christianity) to a literal interpretation of the Bible and the eventual establishment of the Jewish State. The regathering of Israel is a Jewish movement, but it has been encouraged and aided along the way by Bible-believing Christians. On May 14, 1948, the elusive dream of a Jewish homeland in Palestine finally became a reality. The nation of Israel was born!

Chapter 3

Here Come the Russians!

With the development of Zionism and the ruin of the twentieth century, profound prophecies began to be fulfilled. There have been wars and rumors of wars. In 1914, nations rose against nations and kingdoms against kingdoms.

In 1939, the whole scenario began all over again—two world wars have shaken humanity, but unfortunately it will not stop there. A greater war looms on the horizon. Matthew 24:7 describes the scene: "For nation shall rise against nation, and kingdom: and there shall be famines, and pestilences, and earthquakes, in divers places."

The winter of 1918 saw history's first worldwide disease, and 1945 saw mankind's first worldwide famine.

The Rapture of the church is a sign-less event. No one knows what other events will be occurring at the same time. I believe, however, that the Rapture will occur either at or before the beginning of the Tribulation period. It could occur, by the way, today! When it does, we are told that the trumpet of God will sound, the voice of the archangel will herald His coming, and, as thief in the night, Jesus Christ will snatch His bride away! "For this we say ... by the word of the Lord, that we which are alive and remain unto the coming of the Lord shall not prevent them which are asleep" (1 Thessalonians 4:15). In a moment, in a twinkling of an eye we shall be transported to heaven.

Then will begin seven years of unparalleled disaster called in Bible prophecy the Tribulation period. "Alas! For that day is great, so that none is like it: it is even the time of Jacob's trouble; but he shall be saved out of it" (Jeremiah 30:7). Jeremiah reveals the purpose of the Tribulation period. He calls it a time of Jacob's trouble—especially designed for the Jew. It is a part of God's judgment upon His chosen people for their ancient unbelief, and along with the beginning of the Tribulation period, Bible prophecy seems to teach that the battle of Gog and Magog will occur.

The discovery of several large stockpiles of Soviet weapons by the Israeli army in Lebanon at the time of their 1982 invasion appears to be only the tip of the iceberg of Russia's secret war preparations. Documents were also discovered by the Israeli army which laid out in detail a planned Russian invasion of the Middle East which some say had been scheduled for the spring of 1983. According to the *Jerusalem Post*, some $1.7 billion worth of military equipment supplies were found by the Israeli Defense Forces—stashed away in homes, basements, and caves in southern Lebanon. Some estimates range as high as $8 billion worth of Soviet arms.

Israeli intelligence is among the best in the world, and yet they did not expect to find that much military equipment. According to earlier estimates, Israeli intelligence sources expected to find enough military supplies to equip a single division of soldiers. Instead, they found enough to equip ten divisions. So many supplies were found that if the PLO were the only army fighting against Israel, it would take twenty years to use up that much war material.

On September 25, 1980, forty-one Russian ships moved into the Gulf of Aqaba and began to unload military supplies at the Jordanian docks near the port of Eilat. This was reported in the British press but was denied by our State Department. The official view of the United States was that there were no Russian ships there at all. Within two days, however, the number of Russian ships swelled to sixty-seven. That was late September 1980.

Eight months later, by May 15, 1981, some 531 Russian ships had unloaded military supplies at the Jordanian port in the Gulf of Aqaba. Four months later (by September 22, 1981), 1,130 Russian ships had unloaded military supplies.

The seaport at Aqaba, Jordan played host to hundreds of weapons-filled Soviet ships in the early 1980s.

Can you imagine the vast quantity of military hardware and ammunition which was delivered to the Jordanian port by the Soviet Union? Obviously, the weapons found by the Israelis in southern Lebanon represented just a fraction of those unloaded. It is reported that there are six other locations within the countries of Jordan and Syria where the Soviet Union has stored huge quantities of military supplies in preparation for their future invasion of Israel and the Middle East.

According to the Russians, those military supplies unloaded in the Gulf of Aqaba were destined for Iraq for use in its war with Iran. It is believed, however, that at least some of those weapons never reached Iraq, but are stored instead in Jordan and Syria awaiting the day when Russian troops would be air-lifted on a massive scale into the area.

Among those military supplies, there were an estimated thirty thousand Russian tanks and armored vehicles. It appears that war preparations for the prophetic battle of Gog and Magog have been under way since September of 1980. Perhaps the Iran-Iraq war was created by the Soviet Union not only to destabilize the oil-rich countries of the Middle East, but also to create a diversion while these military supplies were readied for use.

When the Russians began their operation unloading military supplies in the Gulf of Aqaba, King Hussein explained to his countrymen that the supplies would be used to "solve the Palestinian problem." Obviously, this was his way of assuring the Palestinians that the weapons would be used against Israel.

Bani-Sadr, the exiled ex-president of Iran, once commented

on the Iran-Iraq war and its connection with the Israeli siege of Beirut. When asked whether the Iran-Iraq conflict or the Israeli incursion into Lebanon had more significance for the Middle East, he replied, "It's the same war."

Even among our military experts the question is not WILL the Russia invade the Middle East, but WHEN and to what extent? The armed services of our country are presently being prepared for war in the Middle East.

The final authority on the battle of Gog and Magog is the Bible, and it is possible that we may be at that point in history. If the world is about to embark upon the Tribulation period, then it is fitting for us to consider what could happen next.

According to the prophets of the Bible, a future worldwide political insanity will grip the nations for seven years. During that time, there will be wars and rumors of wars, concluding with the awesome Armageddon.

Over the years, some theologians have believed that the battle of Gog and Magog and the battle of Armageddon are one and the same battle. Most of the prophets seemed to link them together with descriptions of the one being like the descriptions of the other.

For instance, Ezekiel 39:17 makes a reference to the birds that will come to eat the flesh of the slain on the battlefield. This same description is given of the battle of Armageddon in Revelation 19:17. Is it the same scene, or is it different? In Ezekiel 38, no mention is made 200 million soldiers from the kings of the East. Yet in Revelation 16 there is no mention of Meshech, Tubal, Persia, Ethiopia, Libya, Gomer, or Togarmah.

In fact, Revelation's account of the battle of Gog and Magog places it at the end of the thousand-year millennial reign of Christ. This can only be somewhat frustrating for the student of Bible prophecy. How do we wade through all the menagerie of prophetic scriptures concerning the battles of the end-time? And how do we decipher or discern the chronology of those events?

Well, may I say that it seems the prophets were not concerned with the chronological order of events. They wrote as the Holy Spirit moved upon them. The study of those prophecies represents a pattern of events. However, in the final analysis they bear out the truth of our Savior's admonition when He said, "But of that day and hour knoweth no man, no, not the angels of heaven, but my Father only" (Matthew 24:36).

It has been my opinion that the battle of Gog and Magog will introduce the Tribulation period and that the battle of Armageddon will conclude those seven years. There are some, however, who believe that the battle of Gog and Magog will come in the middle of the Tribulation period, at which time the abomination of desolation will occur. They believe it will kick off that last three and one-half years which the Bible calls "great tribulation" and will culminate with that dreaded battle of Armageddon.

The reason I believe the battle of Gog and Magog will introduce the seven-year Tribulation period is found in Ezekiel 39:9: "And they that dwell in the cities of Israel shall go forth, and shall set on fire and burn the weapons, both the shields and the bucklers, the bows and the arrows, and the handstaves, and the spears, and they shall burn them with fire seven years."

When the battle of Gog and Magog is over, there will be a seven-year period of time for the burning of the weapons. I believe those seven years coincide with the seven years of the Tribulation period. Furthermore, those seven years could hardly be called "tribulation" without some kind of trouble unlike anything that has ever before befallen the human race.

Therefore, it has been my conclusion that a worldwide nuclear war perpetrated by Russia will introduce the last seven years of world history just before that golden age when the kingdom of heaven will be established upon the earth.

There are some who believe that Russia will invade Israel twice. They get this from Ezekiel 38:4: "And I will turn thee back, and put hooks into thy jaws, and I will bring thee forth, and all thine army. ..." According to some, God will first turn back the Russian army, and then a second time will bring them forth for their final destruction. It is my opinion that Ezekiel 38–39 cover the wars of the seven-year Tribulation period. There may well be more than one. In fact, there may be more than two. All these theories contain elements of truth. Which one is absolutely accurate is yet to be proven. However, it is exciting to study the great scriptures concerning these events and to attempt to draw from them a scenario of what will happen and in what order.

It is possible that by the time we get to Ezekiel 39:17–20, the world will have concluded seven years of great devastation—at which time God will invite the birds of the air and the beasts of the field to eat the flesh of the slain.

> And, thou son of man, thus saith the Lord God; Speak unto every feathered fowl, and to every beast of the field, Assemble yourselves, and come; gather yourselves on every side to my sacrifice that I do sacrifice for you, even a great sacrifice upon the mountains of Israel, that ye may eat flesh, and drink blood. Ye shall eat the flesh of the mighty, and drink the blood of the princes of the earth, of rams, of lambs, and of goats, of bullocks, all of them fatlings of Bashan. And ye shall eat fat till ye be full, and drink blood till ye be drunken, of my sacrifice which I have sacrificed for you. Thus ye shall be filled at my table with horses and chariots, with mighty men, and with all men of war, saith the Lord God.

This description must surely be that of Armageddon, for in v. 21, God said: "And I will set my glory among the heathen, and all the heathen shall see my judgment that I have executed, and my hand that I have laid upon them." God has promised in this verse that He will *set His glory among the nations.* I believe this refers to the coming of the Messiah, the Lord Jesus Christ. In the following verses, God laid out His reason for punishing the Jewish people down through the centuries.

> So the house of Israel shall know that I am the Lord their God from that day and forward. And the heathen shall know that the house of Israel went into captivity for their iniquity: because they trespassed against me, therefore hid I my face from them, and gave them into the hand of their enemies: so fell they all

> by the sword. According to their uncleanness and according to their transgressions have I done unto them, and hid my face from them.
>
> —Ezekiel 39:22–24

Why have the Israeli people suffered down through the centuries? Because of their iniquity. Why did the Babylonians destroy Solomon's Temple, and the Romans destroy Herod's Temple? Because the people of Israel trespassed against God. Why did the Romans empty the land of its people in the year A.D. 135 and scatter them throughout the nations of the world to wander for more than eighteen hundred years? Because they had sinned against God. Why will they yet suffer the horrors of the Tribulation period, including the battle of Armageddon? Verse24: "According to their uncleanness and according to their transgressions have I done unto them, and hid my face from them."

These verses teach about the conclusion of seven years called Tribulation and the establishment of the kingdom. Therefore, it is my opinion that Russia will invade Israel at or near the beginning of the Tribulation period, which will be concluded with the great battle of Armageddon. They could be different battles in the same war.

When Isaiah wrote in 14:31 of his book that there would come from the north a smoke, he was referring, I believe, to the great wars of the end-time. I think the key to the prophecy is that word "north." And there are other prophetic scriptures which also describe an invasion from the north. Generally, these scriptures seem to be referring to the great wars of the end-time, including the Russian invasion of Israel. For instance, in Jeremiah 1:13–15 the prophet wrote:

> And the word of the Lord came unto me the second time, saying, What seest thou? And I said, I see a seething pot; and the face thereof is toward the north. Then the Lord said unto me, Out of the north an evil shall break forth upon all the inhabitants of the land. For, lo, I will call all the families of the kingdoms of the north, saith the Lord; and they shall come, and they shall set everyone his throne at the entering of the gates of Jerusalem, and against all the walls thereof round about, and against all the cities of Judah.

These verses seem to represent the Russian invasion of Israel and will lead up to a siege of the city of Jerusalem which I believe will set the stage for the abomination of desolation. Again, Jeremiah 4:6 says: "Set up the standard toward Zion: retire, stay not: for I will bring evil from the north, and a great destruction."

Again, in Jeremiah 6:22: "Thus saith the Lord, Behold, a people cometh from the north country, and a great nation shall be raised from the sides of the earth."

And yet again, in Jeremiah 10:22: "Behold, the noise of the bruit [new] is come, and a great commotion out of the north country, to make the cities of Judah desolate. ..."

When the prophet Micah spoke of the last great series of wars, he wrote in his book: "... the day of thy watchman and thy visitation cometh, now shall be their perplexity" (Micah 7:4). The word *watchman* comes from a Hebrew word which some have translated *north*. The *Jerusalem Bible* translates the verse this way: "Today will come their ordeal from the north, now is the time for their confusion." Indeed, it will be an "ordeal" when the Russians come over the hill.

The prophet Joel also described the invasion of a northern army when he wrote in Joel 2:20: "But I will remove far off from you the northern army, and will drive him into a land barren and desolate, with his face toward the east sea, and his hinder part toward the utmost sea, and his stink shall come up, and his ill savour shall come up, because he hath done great things." Many Bible scholars believe this verse to be a description of the battle of Gog and Magog.

Ezekiel may have been describing that future battle when he saw the spectacular events at the beginning of his book. Ezekiel 1:4: "And I looked, and, behold, a whirlwind came out of the north, a great cloud, and a fire infolding itself, and a brightness was about it, and out of the midst thereof as the colour of amber, out of the midst of the fire."

Zechariah seemed to be referring to the end time when he wrote in Zechariah 6:8: "Then cried he upon me, and spake unto me, saying, Behold, these that go toward the north country have quieted my spirit in the north country."

Finally, the prophet Daniel seemed to link the battle of Gog and Magog to that of Armageddon when he referred to the Antichrist in Daniel 11:44–45: "But tidings out of the east and out of the NORTH shall trouble him: therefore he shall go forth with great fury to destroy, and utterly to make away many. And he shall plant the tabernacles of his palace between the seas in the glorious holy mountain; yet he shall come to his end, and none shall help him." "Tidings out of the north" may be a reference to the Russian invasion, and "tidings out of the east" may be a reference to the awesome Armageddon.

All these verses appear to describe the wars of the Tribulation in general terms. Very few specifics are given. Therefore, we must leave the unfolding of the events in the hands of God. We can only speculate as to what will happen next, but I believe we can say with a fair degree of accuracy that the darkest hour of world history is upon us. The world is soon to see the Russian invasion of Israel and the unfolding of the last seven years of world history.

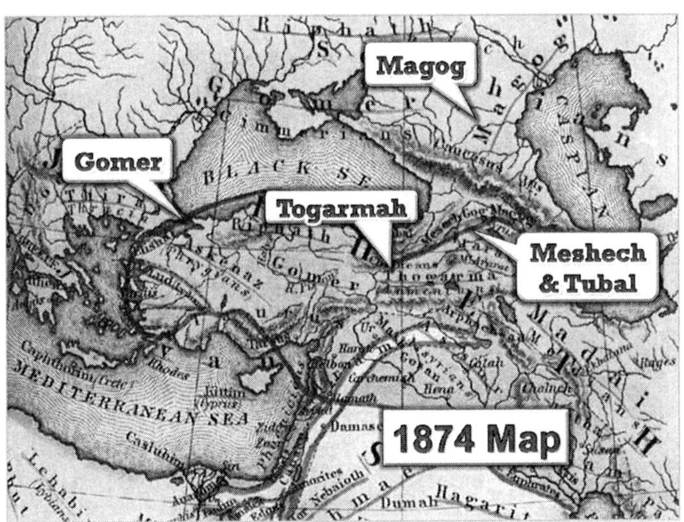

Map from 1874 clearly showing references to GOG and MAGOG in various parts of what is today, Russia.

Students of prophecy all over the world are anxiously awaiting to see what Russia will do in the months ahead. Is the battle of Gog and Magog about to begin? Well, when it does, all Christians will have either been raptured or will be about to be raptured—taken into heaven by Jesus Christ for safety.

Though we do not know exactly when that great event will occur, may I urge you, dear Christian, to win as many people to Christ as you can while you can, for the time is short.

And to you who do not know Jesus Christ as your personal Lord and Savior, may I urge you to turn to Him right now.

Bow your head and pray a simple prayer. Repent of your sins and receive Jesus Christ as your personal Lord and Savior so that you might be saved from these great devastations which shall inevitably come upon an unbelieving human race.

Chapter 4

Four Horsemen Plague the Earth

Once the Rapture has occurred and the battle of Gog and Magog has begun, the Tribulation period will be introduced. According to Bible prophecy, the little nation of Israel will destroy the Russian bear. It will be a bloody time, however, when a fourth of the population of our world will die. There are indications in the Bible that nuclear weapons will be used in the destruction of Gog and Magog. If so, you can imagine how devastating it will be to the

Four Horsemen of the Apocalypse by Victor Vasnetsov (1887)

human race. It will be a time more horrible than history has ever witnessed. Not only will hundreds of millions of people die, but hundreds of millions more will be hurt, maimed, and scarred for life as the Four Horsemen of the Apocalypse thunder across the face of the earth, wreaking their devastation.

The sixth chapter of the book of Revelation gives us the story of the Four Horsemen of the Apocalypse. The Apostle John, who was exiled to the island of Patmos in the latter years of his life, was taken in the spirit into heaven and there was given a vision of the future. John was told of the seven-year Tribulation period, a time of war, of desperation, of desolation—a series of wars where a half of the population of earth will die. The Four Horsemen of the Apocalypse in chapter 6 tell a very interesting story. They are symbols given to reveal to us in the simple language of John's day the events that shall come to pass in the days before the return of Christ.

Deceiver

The term horse is used as a symbol of a conqueror. We shall call the rider of the first horse the "Deceiver." John wrote: "And I saw, and behold a white horse: and he that sat on him had a bow: and a crown was given unto him: and he went forth conquering, and to conquer" (Revelation 6:2).

John described the first as a white horse and the rider upon that horse going forth to conquer. Now, there are some people who may look upon the rider of the white horse as the Lord Jesus Christ. But not so! This rider is not Jesus—far from it! The rider on this white horse is the Deceiver, called by John in his earlier epistle the Antichrist. There is coming one day, perhaps soon, a super-man, a man who will be honored by the governments of this world as the apparent savior of mankind—Mr. Wonderful. He will become the leader of a one-world economic and political system. I believe this one-world system is coming soon. I believe we live in the days just before the return of Jesus Christ.

You know, this past century has known more war and bloodshed than all of the past sixty-one centuries combined. For instance, in World War I there were 8 million casualties. In World War II, there were 78 million casualties. Then there are the millions who have died in the Korean conflict, the Vietnam conflict, and the other wars around the world in this past century. But in all the wars of all of history there have been counted a total of 200 million casualties. Actually, the casualties of this century alone constitute sixty percent of all deaths in all of the wars of history. The politicians are crying, "Peace, peace." But there is no peace, and there will be no peace until the Prince of Peace comes.

A European statesman a few years ago made the statement, "I am looking for someone who can bring peace to this troubled world." He said, "I want to find somebody who can offer a panacea for the problems of this world." And then he said, "I am willing to follow him even if that person be the devil himself." Now we know that the Bible tells of such a man; he is called by John the Antichrist (1 John 2:18). He refers to that terminology in 1 John 2:22 and 1 John 4:2–3, and in his second epistle, 2 John 7.

Now, there are three reasons why I believe this man on the

white horse, the First Horseman of the Apocalypse, is not the Lord Jesus Christ. First of all, he is not the Lamb. The Lamb is seen in the previous chapter as breaking the seals of the scroll—the title deed to the earth. The Lamb, according to John 1:29, is Jesus Christ. John the Baptist pointed to Jesus one day and said, "Behold the Lamb of God, which taketh away the sin of the world" (John 1:29). And the Lamb in Revelation 5 is the One who breaks the seven seals upon the scroll in His hand. If He is the Lamb breaking the first seal, then He cannot be the rider of the first horse in that first seal.

The second reason why I believe this person is not Jesus, but the Antichrist, the Deceiver, is that he has a bow in his hand. The bow appears to have no arrow. Perhaps the arrow has been spent. He goes forth conquering and to conquer. He is coming in to become the so-called savior of the world through war and destruction. This seven-year Tribulation period shall begin, I believe, with a great cataclysmic war—one of the worst wars of history—and will climax in the war of Armageddon at the end of the seven years. Remember, the arrow has been spent, and the bow is in his hand. Jesus, on the other hand, will not need a weapon when He comes. The Bible tells us in Isaiah 11:4 that He will slay the wicked with the breath of His lips. Jesus will not need a bow.

My third reason for believing the rider on the white horse is not the Lord Jesus Christ is because a crown was given unto this rider. The word crown in this second verse is the Greek word *stephonus*. Now, there are two words for crown in the Bible—*stephonus* and *diadem*. A *stephonus* is a conqueror's crown. It always deals with humanity. The second Greek word, *diadem,* always deals with deity. That is the crown that Jesus one day will wear. The rider on this horse has a *stephonus*—a conqueror's crown—a crown taken by him through war. The *stephonus* crown deals with humanity; it is not a *diadem* like that of Revelation 19. And so, I believe the rider on this white horse is the Antichrist that shall emerge one day upon the world scene.

The Jews today are looking forward to the coming of a messiah, and according to all indications, they will accept the Antichrist as their messiah, and a Tribulation temple of sorts will be built. The temple, then, will be usurped by the Antichrist, and the Bible tells us about it in 2 Thessalonians 2. Paul wrote to the church at Thessalonica because they had problems. They may have thought they were in the Tribulation period. So, Paul wrote to them and tried to correct them—to correct the problem. He assured them that the church would not go through the Tribulation. Those who believe in the Lord Jesus Christ will be raptured out of this world before the Antichrist is revealed. The apostle Paul wrote: "... be not soon shaken in mind, or be troubled, neither by spirit, nor by word, nor by letter as from us, as that the day of Christ is at hand. Let no man deceive you by any means: for that day shall not come, except there come a falling away first ..." (2 Thessalonians 2:2–3).

Now, the word for falling away here is the Greek word *apostasia*. The word *apostasia* means departure. It is used by some who believe that the apostasy pictures a great falling away from the truth of the Word of God, and indeed, in many places it does mean that. But the word used in this verse could well refer to the snatching away, or the departure of all believers. After that happens, then "... that man of sin shall be revealed, the son of perdition" (2 Thessalonians 2:3)

He goes on to describe this Antichrist. He said he "... opposeth and exalteth himself above all that is called God, or that is worshiped; so that he as God sitteth in the temple of God, showing himself that he is God."

The Bible goes on to tell us that when the Holy Spirit. "He who now hinders," is taken out of the way, this wicked one shall be revealed. When the Holy Spirit who indwells believers is taken away, you can be sure that all believers will be taken with Him. The Antichrist can then be revealed. His policy of peace is described in 1 Thessalonians 5. It is there we are told that the day of the Lord will come as a thief in the night. "For when they shall say, Peace and safety; then sudden destruction cometh upon them ..." (1 Thessalonians 5:3). The message of the Antichrist will be peace, but there will be only war. Millions of people will die.

Today when Jewish couples recite their marriage vows, the groom takes a glass, puts it on the floor, and with his heel crushes the vessel. This represents the destruction of the Jewish temple in A.D. 70. In so doing, they are looking forward to that day when their Messiah will come and rebuild their temple. When the temple is rebuilt in Jerusalem, the Antichrist will be revealed, and the seven-year Tribulation period will begin.

Destroyer

Then John the apostle describes the rider on the second horse (Revelation 6:4): "And there went out another horse that was red:

and power was given to him that sat thereon to take peace from the earth, and that they should kill one another: and there was given unto him a great sword."

The second horse of the apocalypse is the red horse. I call this one the Destroyer. This is a picture of war—war and desolation—a great destruction—war such as has never been known in the history of mankind. Now there have been many wars in history. In the past six thousand years of recorded history there have been less than 268 years of peace. History is littered with the bodies of the slain. But in this great war, which I believe begins the Tribulation period, a fourth of the population of earth will die. Over a billion people will die. This coming war will be more devastating than any war of history, including World War II.

According to the description of Revelation, this war will be nuclear in nature. Matthew 24 and Revelation 6 are parallel. You could lay one chapter beside the other and read them both together and be able to understand those vivid descriptions of the seven years of Tribulation. Matthew 24 tells us that there shall be wars and rumors of wars. Nation shall rise against nation, kingdom against kingdom. This is a description of the Second Horseman of the Apocalypse. The Bible tells us here that there are two things about this red horseman that we should notice. First of all, his purpose is to take peace from the earth. What a picture of our world today. There is no peace. The communists are bent on taking over the world, and they don't care who they must kill to get it. As we discovered earlier, Russia, who oddly enough is symbolized by the color red, is building up her armaments, moving her troops, and preparing for aggression. War in the Middle East is building. The communists in China say they are willing to lose 700 million of their population in order to rule the world. They are taking peace from the earth. The purpose of the rider on the red horse is to take peace away.

The second thing I want you to see is his program. His program is the sword. The Bible says, "There was given unto him a great sword." While men are looking for peace, they are arming themselves for war. There will be a time when the world will erupt into a cataclysmic war, a holocaust such as has never been known before. We are headed for war. Back in the days of ancient Israel in the book of 2 Chronicles, the Bible says that there was no teaching priest, that they were without law, they were without the Word of God. Because of that, the verse says, there was no peace anywhere. As was the picture then, so it is today. We live in a society that is actually burning around us. One evangelist put it this way. He said, "The world is on fire, and Mr. Complacency sits in his easy chair and does not realize that the world is burning down around us." The crime rate is rising; there are more murders today, more rapes, more robberies than have ever been before. The late Dag Hammarskjold, secretary general of the United Nations, sat in his office one day and wept as he said, "We have tried so hard for peace, and yet we have failed so miserably." The rider on this second horse is the Destroyer. His job—to take peace from the earth.

According to Bible prophecy, he lives in Mystery Babylon—a city and/or a nation that has not been named in the Bible but is simply given the title "Mystery Babylon." From his great city he shall wield influence over the ten-nation European confederation formed in an effort to establish a world government with a one-world monetary system. Now, it is the opinion of many that some of the ten of the nations which today comprise the European Union represent the fulfillment of that Bible prophecy. If so, we may be very near to the Rapture of the church and the beginning of the Tribulation period.

The Euro—the currency of the European Union—with a woman riding a beast.

"And in his estate shall stand up a vile person, to whom they shall not give the honour of the kingdom: but he shall come in peaceably, and obtain the kingdom by flatteries" (Daniel 11:21). According to this verse, he will not become the president of the United States of Europe; he will not be given the honor of the kingdom. However, he shall have control of that Revived Roman Empire from a behind-the-scenes manipulation.

As the Tribulation period progresses, Mr. Antichrist will attempt to control communications and transportation. He will set about to solve the problems of famine and starvation through the control of food distribution, energy supplies, and the establishment of a new monetary system.

By the middle of the Tribulation period, however, he will introduce an image of the beast through which he will control the world's monetary system and will require a mark to be made either in the hand or the forehead of every person in the world. It will be necessary for people to accept the mark in order to be able to buy or sell.

The introduction of the mark could occur somewhere before the middle of the Tribulation period, so that by the end of the first three and one-half years of his leadership, his Mystery Babylon will have fallen into ill favor with the ten-nation European confederation. This Revived Roman Empire, called in the Bible a beast with seven heads and ten horns, will turn upon Mystery Babylon and destroy the great city with fire. Unfortunately, the Antichrist will escape the holocaust and move his government to Jerusalem.

There seems to be a power play at this point in Bible prophecy, for the Antichrist will seek to establish Jerusalem as his world capital. When he arrives in Israel and Jerusalem, he will proceed to the Temple Mount. He will enter the Jewish sanctuary, stop the sacrifices, and proclaim himself to be God.

The ten-nation European confederation will have other thoughts about that, however, and the rest of the world will concur. By this time, it will appear to the world that they have been made slaves by this world ruler, and in my opinion, they will blame his people, the Jews. Anti-Semitism will be at its worst, and all the nations of the world will gather their armies to converge upon Israel for the genocide of the Jews.

The last three and one-half years of the seven are referred to as the Great Tribulation. This three and one-half–year period will be filled with natural disasters—earthquakes, wild weather, famine, and drought. Floods and violent storms will become commonplace. Even the sun and the moon will be affected.

Drought

The Apostle John records for us the rider on the third horse. The Third Horseman of the Apocalypse is Drought. Another word could be Famine. This world is going hungry. There are many who are going to bed each night without anything to eat. There are children starving by the millions in various parts of this world. The twenty-eight countries that surround the equatorial belt of the earth are actually being turned into a dust bowl. Revelation 6:5–6:

> And when he had opened the third seal, I heard the third beast say, Come and see. And I beheld, and lo a black horse; and he that sat on him had a pair of balances in his hand. And I heard a voice in the midst of the four beasts say, A measure of wheat for a penny, and three measures of barley for a penny; and see thou hurt not the oil and the wine.

Around 9 million people die each year because of famine. Each year that number grows. The statistics continue to climb. In many parts of the world, drought is creating famine. Elsewhere, inflation is creating famine. The annual rate of inflation in the Unites States is about 8.3 percent. That doesn't sound too bad until we realize at that rate prices will quadruple every twenty years. Inflation has eaten away and will continue to eat away our dollar.

An article in *U.S. News and World Report* said that the year

"A measure of wheat for a penny, and three measures of barley for a penny..."

marked the beginning of a new era—the era of famine. The greatest cause of famine has been the astounding increase in the population of our world. There are over seven billion people on our planet today. There is obviously not enough food to feed the starving millions. Note the message, please, of this verse: "A measure of wheat for a penny, and three measures of barley for a penny ..." (Revelation 6:6).

A penny in the days of John was considered a day's wages, and a measure of wheat was considered one day's food supply for one person. What an incredible picture of our world in the days ahead!

At the beginning of the Tribulation period, the battle of Gog and Magog will have introduced nuclear destruction. In the middle of the Tribulation period, the downfall of Mystery Babylon could bring yet another nuclear disaster, and it seems that during the last half of the Tribulation period, those nuclear wars will have affected the sun, the moon, and the planets—perhaps even the orbit of the earth about the sun.

> ... the foundations of the earth do shake. The earth is utterly broken down, the earth is clean dissolved, the earth is moved exceedingly. The earth shall reel to and fro like a drunkard, and shall be removed like a cottage; and the transgression thereof shall be heavy upon it; and it shall fall, and not rise again. And

> it shall come to pass in that day, that the Lord shall punish the host of the high ones that are on high, and the kings of the earth upon the earth. And they shall be gathered together, as prisoners are gathered in the pit, and shall be shut up in the prison, and after many days shall they be visited. Then the moon shall be confounded, and the sun ashamed, when the Lord of hosts shall reign in mount Zion, and in Jerusalem, and before his ancients gloriously.
>
> —Isaiah 24:18–23

Yes, the last three and one-half years of that seven-year Tribulation will be the most devastating ever faced by the human race. Matthew 24:21–22: "For then shall be great tribulation, such as was not since the beginning of the world to this time, no, nor ever shall be. And except those days should be shortened, there should no flesh be saved. ..."

Death

Returning to the book of Revelation, John describes the rider on the fourth horse: "And I looked, and behold a pale horse: and his name that sat on him was Death, and Hell followed with him. And power was given unto them over the fourth part of the earth, to kill with sword, and with hunger, and with death, and with the beasts of the earth" (Revelation 6:8).

The Fourth Horseman of the Apocalypse is Death. The word *pale* here refers to sort of a green color, a ghoulish color, the color of a corpse or the color of leprosy. This horseman tells the gruesome story that a fourth of the population of earth will die. World War II brought a death toll of 78 million people. In World War I, 8 million people died. The Bible describes a companion which travels with death—one who conquers. The Bible says Hell followed with him. People who die during that war will be unbelievers. They will be cast into hell without hope, without God for eternity. In fact, Isaiah 5:14 reports that hell shall enlarge itself because of the billions of people who will die.

Chapter 5

Inevitable Armageddon

The events of those last three and one-half years of the Tribulation period are almost in describable. Another one-third of the population of the earth will die. Adding the one-fourth of earth's population who will die at the beginning of the Tribulation period to the one-third of the earth's population who die in the last half of the Tribulation period, makes exactly one-half of the people of our planet who will die during whose seven years.

The battle of Armageddon is described in the Bible as being

Modern Jerusalem is a very complex, layered, mix of things both modern and ancient; Jewish, Christian, and Islamic.

the most devastating war of history. All the nations of the world will send their armies to Israel. In my opinion, their aim will be the genocide of the Jew. Not one nation will be allied with Israel. Not one will stand by their side. Not one will send them military aid.

According to the book of the Revelation, 200 million soldiers will be fielded by the kings of the East, and it is noteworthy, I think, that in 1964 Mao Tse-tung boasted that he could field an army of 200 million men. In addition to those soldiers from China and the Far Eastern nations, there will be soldiers from Europe, Africa, South and Central America, and yes, perhaps even from the United States itself. The outlook will be pretty bleak for the Israeli army.

During past wars with the Arabs, the Israelis were outnumbered thirty to one, but in this last great war of history, Israel will be outnumbered at least a thousand times that, and the battle will go badly for Jerusalem. According to the prophetic description given in the book of Zechariah, the city of Jerusalem will be made a cup of trembling unto all nations. Zechariah 12:2: "Behold, I will make Jerusalem a cup of trembling unto all the people round about, when they shall be in the siege both against Judah and against Jerusalem."

In the height of the battle, half the city will fall to the enemy. Two-thirds of the land will be cut off or taken from the Jews. When the city of Jerusalem is surrounded, the houses will be rifled, and the women ravaged. Seemingly, there will be no way out for the Jews. They will be running out of ammunition and running out of time. It will be a time of despair. Within a matter of hours, the last great assault will be made, and the Jewish people will be overrun. Soon every Jew on the face of the earth will die. The world will finally be rid of the Jew— or so it will seem.

Zechariah 12:3 covers the action of the war and gives in ominous tones the perennial hazards of making war on Jerusalem and Israel: "And in that day will I make Jerusalem a burdensome stone for all people: All that burden themselves with it shall be cut in pieces, though all the people of the earth be gathered against it." All those who tangle with Jerusalem will be "cut in pieces" indeed, and then some! Despite the best efforts of the world's most capable and fanatic invaders through four thousand years of bloody conflict, Jerusalem has survived, and it will continue to survive.

The armies of the world will come together to do their fearsome work in the valley of Megiddo in quiet Galilee. In that valley, "called in the Hebrew tongue Armageddon," untold millions of soldiers armed with the ultimate weapons of war will stage mankind's most effective attempt at suicide. Blood will flow, according to Revelation 14:20 "up to the bridles of the horses."

Jerusalem, nearly one hundred miles away from the combat zone, will not be spared the effects of this horrifying conflict. Zechariah 14:2 laments: "The city shall be taken, and the houses rifled, and the women ravished; and half of the city shall go forth into captivity."

Considering the pure numbers of the invading forces, no portion of little Israel will be safe from actual combat. And Jerusalem, God's city, veteran of invasions, rapings, and lootings from time immemorial, will have to endure this one last catastrophe. But in this final hour of terrible conflict, something miraculous will transpire among the people of Israel. Pressed to the wall—with their Promised Land torn apart by a vicious war, with their historic fears of national annihilation coming to reality before their eyes—the Jews turn to God. They have always done this, but in this case, they turn to their Messiah at last! It seems that the testimonies of the 144.000 Hebrew Christians who minister on earth after the Rapture and who share their faith in Christ, at last get a hearing in Israel.

Jesus said clearly enough in John 14:6: "No man cometh unto the father, but by me."

In a time when their need for divine help is greater than ever before, the Jewish people will turn to their native Son, the Carpenter of Nazareth. Jesus will be accepted as the true Messiah of Israel.

Isaiah 53 (the conscience of the Jewish people) will be read with a new understanding in Israel: "He is despised and rejected of men; a man of sorrows and acquainted with grief: and we hid as it were our faces from him; he was despised, and we esteemed him not ... But he was wounded for our transgressions, he was bruised for our iniquities" (Isaiah 53:3, 5).

Whether out of the desperation of that tragic moment, or from the testimony of Christian witnesses, or from a national realization that disaster has ever followed the Jews since the time of the crucifixion, the Jewish nation will completely awaken to Christ. They will finally declare, "Blessed is He who comes in the name of the Lord!"

This is the password to salvation for the Jews. Jesus told them while He was on the subject of the destruction of Jerusalem (Matthew 23:37–39) that He would not return until they welcomed Him in the words of Psalm 118:26: "Blessed is he that cometh in the name of the Lord."

It will be the greatest spiritual awakening in all of history as the Jewish people come to Christ by the millions. It will be a true day of atonement in Israel as Zechariah prophesies: "In that day there shall be a fountain opened to the house of David and to the inhabitants of Jerusalem for sin and uncleanness" (Zechariah 13:1).

Also, Romans 11:26 says: "And so all Israel will be saved."

God is practical. He promised deliverance to Israel when the nation was faithful. He demonstrated this by bringing His chosen out of Egypt with a miraculous deliverance in the time of Moses. He will do no less in the time of the Armageddon.

The Jewish people will receive Christ in the midst of battle. There is no time to build a lot of churches or to ponder a lot of Scripture when Armageddon is going on in your land! The nation is saved, as a nation, instantaneously and on the battlefield. It is as if an electric current of truth is shot through everyone at once.

God's rewards are immediate. The tide of Armageddon will change abruptly as the Lord empowers Israel with newfound military strength. The weakest buck private in the field will fight like King David, and the generals will be like God in battle, as Zechariah 12:8–9 describes it: "In that day shall the Lord defend the inhabitants of Jerusalem: and he that is feeble among them at that day shall be as David; and the house of David shall be as God. And it shall come to pass in that day, that I will seek to destroy all the nations that come against Jerusalem."

At that point, however, in the height of Armageddon, in the thickest of the battle, there will be an astronomical catastrophe. Just as Joshua of old reached up his hand through prayer and pulled the lever of heaven to stop the sun in its place when his troops were fighting for the men of Gibeah, even so the greater Joshua will create what can only be described as another astronomical phenomenon.

Now, please understand that the name Joshua in the Old Testament happens to be the same as the New Testament name of Jesus. Yes, the Son of David will turn out the lights of heaven. The sun will turn as black as sackcloth of ashes, and the moon will turn as blood.

From the eastern sky over Jerusalem there will appear a light—exquisite in its beauty, magnificent in its majesty. Jesus Christ will appear to fulfill the ancient Jewish hope for the coming of their Messiah. Every eye shall see Him, and every knee shall bow, and every tongue shall confess that Jesus is Lord—all to the glory of God.

Revelation 19 describes the coming of Christ for us. John wrote in verses 11–16:

> And I saw heaven opened, and behold a white horse; and he that sat upon him was called Faithful and True, and in righteousness he doth judge and make war. His eyes were as a flame of fire, and on his head were many crowns; and he had a name writ-

> ten, that no man knew, but he himself. And he was clothed with a vesture dipped in blood: and his name is called The Word of God. And the armies which were in heaven followed him upon white horses, clothed in fine linen, white and clean. And out of his mouth goeth a sharp sword, that with it he should smite the nations: and he shall rule them with a rod of iron: and he treadeth the winepress of the fierceness and wrath of Almighty God. And he hath on his vesture and on his thigh a name written, KING OF KINGS AND LORD OF LORDS.

Yes, Jesus Christ will come to save the day. According to the prophet Zechariah: "Then shall the Lord go forth, and fight against those nations, as when he fought in the day of battle. And his feet shall stand in that day upon the Mount of Olives" (Zechariah 14:3–4).

Jesus will return to His beloved Mount of Olives, adjacent to the Jerusalem temple site, where He used to retire in the evenings for prayer. Cataclysmic things will happen. Militarily, those who attacked Jerusalem are in for a bad time of it, to say the least. Zechariah 14:12 says: "The Lord will smite all the people that have fought against Jerusalem; their flesh shall consume away while they stand upon their feet, and their eyes shall consume away in their holes, and their tongue shall consume away in their mouth."

Revelation 19 goes on to picture fowls eating the flesh of kings, captains, and mighty men. The Antichrist "and the kings of the earth, and their armies" in verse 19 attempt war with Christ and His heavenly troops with a predictable outcome. John sees no scenes of lengthy battle.

Jesus Christ will put down the armies of the enemy, and Revelation goes immediately to the disposal of the Antichrist and his schemes for world domination. He gets the "lake of fire" in verse 20: "And the beast was taken, and with him the false prophet that wrought miracles before him, with which he deceived them that had received the mark of the beast, and them that worshipped his image. These both were cast alive into a lake of fire burning with brimstone."

The troops of the Antichrist (v. 21) are "slain with the sword of him that sat upon the horse ... and all the fowls were filled with their flesh."

This supernatural ending to the battle of Armageddon is not new in biblical accounts. We may say that there are natural wars and supernatural wars in connection with Jewish history, which is the story of a people whose destiny is controlled by God. The deliverance of the Jews from Egypt showed the loss of the Egyptian

This is the Plain of Esdraelon—an enormous flat region in Israel's north, near ancient Megiddo, where the Bible says the Battle of Armageddon will occur.

forces when they tried to cross the Red Sea on the dry land used by the Jews.

David experienced a supernatural victory over Goliath in response to his faithfulness. Joshua demolished the walls of Jericho with trumpets. The Maccabees experienced the miraculous touch of God when they defeated Antiochus and rededicated the Second Temple.

Armageddon follows suit, a demonstration that God responds to true faith. When the gentile nations first march against the Holy Land, they certainly have no fear of the little Israeli army. They plunder Jerusalem and set up their bloodletting in Galilee, indifferent to the great people whose land they desecrate.

But what a different story when the Jews turn to Christ! How shocking for the gentiles to suddenly face an army of King David's with Jesus Christ at the head of it!

We have heard of supernatural events in Israel's wars with the Arabs, but the final conflict will be the most spectacular and supernatural war in history. On that occasion the issue will be atheism versus faith in God, and as we have seen, God takes a hand in it. It is a picture a vicious Armageddon.

Armageddon, thankfully, is the end of every kind of war. It marks the return of Jesus to the earth for an extended stay and a new kingdom. The great age of "peace on earth, good will toward men" will be ushered in at the climax of Armageddon, and Jesus Christ will be crowned King of kings and Lord of lords! Our Lord will establish His throne on Mt. Moriah. He will set up His kingdom and rule over the earth for a thousand years. We who have been raptured into heaven seven years earlier will come back to this earth with the Lord. We shall rule and reign with Christ for a thousand years. (The word *millennium* simply means "one thousand.") It will be a golden age for the people of our world.

In that day, the curse will be lifted from the earth, and every crop will be a bumper crop. There will be no thorns on the roses, no weeds in the fields. There will be no wild weather and no wild animals. The lion will lie down with the lamb, and a little child shall lead them. During those thousand years the life expectancy of man will be expanded, and he will be able to live for hundreds of years, as he did in the days before the flood.

There will be an immortal people, I think, living and ruling in this world. But there will also be the survivors of the Tribulation period—those who will be living as we live today in natural bodies not yet redeemed. There will be people born, and there will be those who die. The gospel will be preached, and there will be conversions to the Savior. However, even then salvation will not be mandatory. Man will be free either to accept or reject Jesus Christ as his Lord and Savior.

During this thousand-year period, Satan will be exiled from planet earth. He will not be allowed to come and tempt humanity—until, however, the thousand years come to a close. At the end of the millennium, he will be loosed for a little season and, oddly enough, he will have the power to deceive the nations and bring a great army once again against Jerusalem. It is described in the last chapters of Revelation as another battle of Gog and Magog. But, says the Bible, God will send fire out of heaven to destroy them, and then Satan will be cast into hell to be tormented forever and ever.

At the close of this last great battle which occurs at the end of the millennial reign of Christ, the Great White Throne Judgment will take place. All sinners will be raised to stand before God, and the books will be opened. Every person who during his lifetime has rejected Jesus Christ as his personal Lord and Savior will be judged according to his works. And the verdict? Well, the verdict will be a foregone conclusion. He will stand guilty before God.

At the conclusion of that judgment, every unbeliever will be cast into hell. It will be a sad occasion for all people. Even the saints will weep. How sad that anyone could say no to the God who created him and loved him and gave His Son to die for him.

After the Great White Throne Judgment is completed, the earth and the heavens are dissolved with fire and a new heaven and a new earth will be established. Then that holy city, New Jerusalem, will embark from its journey in the third heaven to the earth. It is a city prepared for you and for me and is described in the last chapters of the book of Revelation. It is a city fifteen hundred miles long, fifteen hundred miles wide, and fifteen hundred miles high.

Its walls are of jasper, its gates are of pearl, and its streets are paved with gold. All tears will be wiped away and all sorrow turned into joy. The holy city, some believe, will orbit the earth, and we shall live in the glory, the beauty, and the majesty of the New Jerusalem with our Savior, the Lord Jesus Christ, for all eternity.

We will not sit around on fleecy clouds plunking on harps.

There will be things to do, jobs to fill. But at this point, it is beyond our mental capacity to comprehend. "Eye hath not seen, nor ear heard, neither have entered into the heart of man the things which God hath prepared for them that love Him" (1 Corinthians 2:9).

"It will be worth it all when we see Jesus. It will be worth it all when we see Christ. One glimpse of His dear face all sorrows will erase. So let us gladly run the race till we see Christ!"

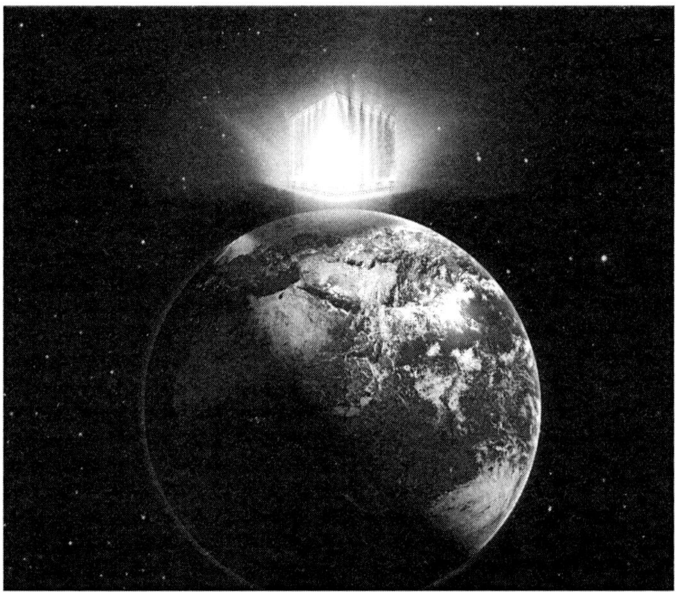

The Bible teaches us in Revelation that New Jerusalem will come down from heaven to the earth — a Holy City prepared for the redeemed, and is described as being about 1,500 miles long, 1,500 miles wide, and 1,500 miles high!

Part 2

A Prophetic Perspective on the High Holy Days

Chapter 1

The Sound of the Trumpet

The resurrection of the saints, the Rapture of the church, and the Second Coming of Christ are all connected with the blowing of a trumpet. In 1 Thessalonians, the Apostle Paul wrote: “For the Lord himself shall descend from heaven with a shout, with the voice of the archangel, and with the trump of God: and the dead in Christ shall rise first: Then we which are alive and remain shall be caught up together with them in the clouds, to meet the Lord in the air: and so shall we ever be with the Lord” (1 Thessalonians 4:16–17).

In 1 Corinthians 15:51–52, Paul wrote: “Behold, I shew you a mystery; We shall not all sleep, but we shall all be changed, In a moment, in the twinkling of an eye, at the last trump: for the trumpet shall sound, and the dead shall be raised incorruptible, and we shall be changed.”

In each of these verses the apostle Paul refers to the trumpet.

The blowing of the trumpet has its origins in Old Testament Judaism. Whether it be the modern use of the trumpet in our military today as in the playing of “Taps” or “Reveille,” or whether it be the charge of the cavalry into battle in days gone by, the trumpet's use finds its origin in the early pages of the Bible. "The eyes of Texas are upon you," says the happy song, "til Gabriel blows his horn."

Yes, the use of the trumpet goes deep in its symbolism. It has a very great spiritual and prophetic significance. Every born-again Christian today who looks forward to the Second Coming of Christ "as a thief in the night" to snatch away His bride is listening for that spine-tingling, exhilarating sound of God's divine trumpet.

Blowing the Rosh Hashanah "shofar"

The ram's horn trumpet is blown each year on Rosh Hashanah, the Jewish New Year. It is called in the Bible the Feast of Trumpets. This Jewish holy day, along with Yom Kippur, the Day of Atonement, and the Feast of Tabernacles, has a very great prophetic significance, for they look forward to that day when Messiah will come, raise the dead, judge the world, and establish His Millennial Kingdom on earth.

There are a total of seven Jewish holy days given through Moses to the Jewish people in Leviticus 23. Those seven Jewish holy days tell the story of God's plan of the ages. The first four feast days have already been fulfilled. They are the Passover, the Feast of Unleavened Bread, the Feast of Firstfruits, and Pentecost, Prophetically, they picture the first coming of Christ and the Holy Spirit. Christ was our Passover Lamb. He fulfilled the Feast of Unleavened Bread through His death and burial. He then fulfilled the Feast of Firstfruits through His resurrection on the first day of the week. Incidentally, He fulfilled these three Jewish holy days in their prophetic significance on the very day of each feast. The Feast of Pentecost was fulfilled also on the exact day of that feast. Its fulfillment is found in the first chapters of the book of Acts, when the Holy Spirit empowered the early church for its great worldwide mission. Thus concludes the first set of holy days.

In John 4:35, Jesus said, "Say not ye, There are yet four months, and then cometh harvest?" There are four months from Pentecost to Rosh Hashanah. These four months, then, represent the Church Age, the dispensation of grace: the time wherein God calls out, for His name, a gentile bride. The last three feasts also have a prophetic significance, but their prophecies are yet to be fulfilled. Rosh Hashanah, or the Feast of Trumpets, which occurs on the first day of the month called Tishri, in late September or early October each year, represents that great day in the future when God's trumpet shall sound, the dead shall be raised, and the judgment set. Following Rosh Hashanah, there are seven Days of Affliction, a time of introspection. They are called the Days of Awe, and they represent the Tribulation period. The tenth day of Tishri is called the Day of Atonement. Prophetically, the Day of

Atonement represents the salvation of the nation of Israel in the height of the battle of Armageddon. It is the time when Messiah comes to save His people. It is a day of repentance for the Jew as he seeks the forgiveness of God for his unbelief. Five days later, the Jewish people move into tents, or tabernacles, to celebrate the Feast of Tabernacles. Prophetically, this represents the millennial reign of Christ when for a thousand years we will rule and reign with Christ on earth.

You see, the three holy days—that of Rosh Hashanah, Yom Kippur, and the Feast of Tabernacles—are yet to find their ultimate fulfillment.

This chapter will provide an in-depth look at the Feast of Trumpets and the Day of Atonement and search out their prophetic significance as found in ancient Judaism. Unlike the other festivals of the Jewish calendar, both Rosh Hashanah and Yom Kippur do not commemorate any historical event in the life of the Jewish nation.

The two festivals are such high holy days that preparation for them actually begins a month earlier on the first of the Jewish month Elul. Each day throughout the month, the ram's-horn trumpet is blown. On the day before Rosh Hashanah (the last day of the month of Elul), no trumpet is blown. The last trumpet is sounded on Rosh Hashanah, the first of Tishri. It is the final trumpet in the series of thirty days of trumpet blowing. The blowing of the shofar on Rosh Hashanah could be the last trump referred to in 1 Corinthians 15:52: "In a moment, in the twinkling of an eye, at the last trump: for the trumpet shall sound, and the dead shall be raised incorruptible, and we shall be changed." This may be that last trumpet.

However, there is another possible interpretation of this verse. When the ram's-horn trumpet is blown on Rosh Hashanah, it is blown in a series of trumpet blasts, some short, some long. Some of the sounds are very short, staccato notes. There is a wailing note that is always preceded and followed by a long clear blast. The wailing or sobbing note is one of three alternatives: three short blasts of the horn, a series of extremely short blasts, or a combination of the two—three short blasts followed by a series of staccato notes. As each is repeated three times, this makes a total of thirty blasts. In addition to the thirty blasts blown before the special Jewish service called the *Musaf*, another sixty blasts are blown during the service. The last *Teki'ah* blast is drawn out, and is called *Teki'ah Gedolah*. It is the great *Teki'ah*. It reminds the people of the long sounding of the horn after God's appearance on Sinai, which signified that the divine presence had gone up from the mountain. That last extremely long sound of the shofar trumpet may be the "last trump" referred to in 1 Corinthians 15:52, a prophetic picture of that day when the dead in Christ shall rise and the living saints shall be caught up with them to meet the Lord in the

Incidentally, the shofar does not have to be a ram's horn. It can be the horn of any clean animal, except for the ox or calf. God refused to allow the Jewish people to use the horn of a calf or an ox because of their worship of the golden calf while Moses was on top of the mountain. Generally, however, a ram's horn is used.

During the month of Elul, a special psalm is recited together with the blowing of the shofar. This is Psalm 27. The psalm opens with a reference to Rosh Hashanah and Yom Kippur. "The Lord is my light and my salvation; whom shall I fear?" The words "my light" are taken to refer to Rosh Hashanah, and the words "my salvation" refer to the Day of Atonement.

Verse 5 continues, "For in the time of trouble he shall hide me in his pavilion: in the secret of his tabernacle shall he hide me. ..." Here is a reference to the Feast of Tabernacles. This psalm is recited daily until the last day of the Feast of Tabernacles is observed. "The Lord is my light," said David, referring to Rosh Hashanah. The light refers to the Shekinah Glory. Remember, it was on that day that Moses and the people of Israel received the Torah from God, and the glory of the Lord came down on the top of Mount Sinai. Moses was allowed to see the back side of God's glory, and when he descended from the mountain on Yom Kippur, the face of Moses glistened with a strange light of God's glory.

Prophetically, the light of Psalm 27 represents a light of understanding which will illuminate the darkened minds of the Jewish people at the beginning of the Tribulation and will climax seven years later with their salvation.

According to the ancient Jewish rabbis, the festival of Rosh Hashanah represents three things: the anniversary of Adam's creation, the future day of judgment, and the future day of renewing the bond between God and Israel.

It was on an ancient Rosh Hashanah that God stooped down and formed Adam from the dust of the ground, breathed into his nostrils, and man became a living soul. Rosh Hashanah is believed to be the sixth day of creation—the day when Adam was created. It is also considered as the birthday of many of God's great patriarchs. Abraham, for instance, is said to have been born on Rosh Hashanah, as well as Isaac, Jacob, and Samuel. According to Bible scholars, Jesus, the Son of God, was born in Bethlehem's stable on Rosh Hashanah, September 29, 4 B.C.—not December 25, as is generally believed today (though He was most probably conceived in the womb of Mary by the Holy Spirit on December 25, 5 B.C., exactly two hundred and eighty days before His birth). Two hundred and eighty days is the perfect gestation period for the birth of a human child.

It was on Rosh Hashanah that Jesus was baptized by John in the Jordan River.

According to the ancient Jewish religion, Rosh Hashanah is also the Day of Judgment. It is that great and terrible Day of the Lord that shall come according to Joel 2:31. That verse is quoted by Peter on the Day of Pentecost: "And I will shew wonders in heaven above, and signs in the earth beneath; blood, and fire, and vapour of smoke: The sun shall be turned into darkness, and the moon into blood, before that great and notable day of the Lord come"(Acts 2:19–20). That "great and notable day" refers to God's judgment upon lost mankind. Many believe it refers to the Tribulation period and uniquely to Armageddon.

Not only do the Jews regard Rosh Hashanah as the day of Adam's creation and the future day of judgment, but they believe that on some future Rosh Hashanah, God will renew His bond with Israel (the seventieth week of Daniel). God's dealing with the Jewish people will be renewed during the Tribulation period, when they will come to repentance and receive Christ as their Messiah. This will be the Day of Atonement for Israel.

The Second Coming of Christ in power and great glory at the height of the battle of Armageddon is the fulfillment of the prophetic Yom Kippur, and will usher in the glorious Feast of Tabernacles, or the millennial reign of Christ.

There's another interesting bit of information about Rosh Hashanah, the Jewish New Year: It is observed for two days, not one. These two days, however, are considered one long day. There's a reason for this. Tradition required that the new month be determined not by mathematical calculation, but by the evidence of eyewitnesses who had seen the new moon. Accordingly, the people would look out for the new moon on the night of the twenty-ninth and the thirtieth. The following day, the thirtieth, the Sanhedrin court would receive the witnesses, and even if they arrived late in the afternoon, they would declare that day to be Rosh Chodesh, the first of the new month. But the Jewish people were scattered throughout other countries of the world, and the Jews in those far-flung countries had no contact with the mother land. Therefore, two days were observed as Rosh Hashanah to ensure that all the Jews throughout the world were observing the same day.

In the same way, we are told by the Savior that men cannot determine the day of Christ's coming by mathematical calculation. We are told to look for the day. It can be determined only by signs in the heavens and on earth as darkness approaches. Ultimately, it will be one very long day—like the day Joshua made the sun stand still at Gibeah.

Interestingly enough, Zechariah talks about that great day: "And it shall come to pass in that day, that the light shall not be clear, nor dark. But it shall be one day which shall be known to the Lord, not day, nor night: but it shall come to pass, that at evening time it shall be light" (Zechariah 14:6–7).

Perhaps the observance of Rosh Hashanah by the Jewish people down through the centuries for a prolonged period of forty-eight hours is a prophetic picture of that unusual day described by Zechariah.

Rosh Hashanah is also pictured as the Day of Judgment. Strangely enough, the zodiac sign of Libra, the scales, rises in the month of Tishri, the very month wherein begins Rosh Hashanah, God's judgment upon mankind. At the synagogue service on Rosh Hashanah, many of the people wear a white garment or some white article of clothing over their Sabbath clothes. It is reminiscent of a shroud and may picture prophetically that day when we receive our robes of righteousness.

In the Bible, Rosh Hashanah is described as a day of sounding the horn. The ram's horn is reminiscent of the ram caught in the thicket which was used by Abraham as a substitute sacrifice for his son, Isaac. Much of the ceremony of the day hinges around that historic event. The central ceremony of the festival is the sounding of the shofar, the ram's horn.

The shofar should be curved, a symbol that man must bend his will before God. It is usually softened and shaped in hot water. There must be no impairment of the sound of the shofar. A split or hole in the shofar is liable to render it unfit. Before blow-

The shofar

ing the shofar, the congregation of Jewish people recites Psalm 47 seven times. This psalm exalts God as King of all the earth, a befitting theme for the blowing of the shofar. It also includes the verse, "God is gone up with a shout, the Lord with the sound of a trumpet" (verse 5). This verse is given as the reason for holding the shofar with the wide end pointing upward. Another six verses are then recited. The first letters of each verse form an acrostic, reading "Kera Satan," which means "tear up Satan." This, of course, is exactly what will happen when God's great future Rosh Hashanah comes.

According to Rabbi Saadiah Gaon, who lived in the ninth century, there are ten reasons for sounding the shofar on Rosh Hashanah:

- *Number 1:* Rosh Hashanah, as the day of creation, is the anniversary of God's rule. It is a coronation day and Israel, as God's people, proclaims His kingship.
- *Number 2:* Rosh Hashanah introduces the seven Days of Penitence, and the shofar calls for repentance.
- *Number 3:* The shofar evokes the revelation at Sinai when the Torah was given to Israel amidst the blowing of the horn.
- *Number 4:* The sound of the shofar is compared to the inspiring message of Ezekiel 33:2–7: "When I bring the sword upon a land, if the people of the land take a man of their coasts, and set him for their watchman: If when he seeth the sword come upon the land, he blow the trumpet, and warn the people; Then whosoever heareth the sound of the trumpet, and taketh

not warning; if the sword come, and take him away, his blood shall be upon his own head. ... But he that taketh warning shall deliver his soul. But if the watchman see the sword come, and blow not the trumpet, and the people be not warned; if the sword come, and take any person from among them, he is taken away in his iniquity; but his blood will I require at the watchman's hand. So thou, O son of man, I have set thee a watchman unto the house of Israel; therefore thou shalt hear the word at my mouth, and warn them from me."

» *Number 5:* The shofar is the sound of battle and the clash of arms. The memory of the capture of Jerusalem and the destruction of the temple evokes prayers for the speedy return of Israel's national glory.
» *Number 6:* The shofar is symbolic of the ram Abraham sacrificed instead of Isaac.
» *Number 7:* The sound of a horn arouses fear. Amos 3:6 says, "Shall a trumpet be blown in the city, and the people not be afraid?"
» *Number 8:* The shofar evokes the ultimate Day of Judgment, as in Zephaniah 1:14, 16: "The great day of the Lord is near, it is near, and hasteth greatly ... A day of the trumpet and alarm. ..."
» *Number 9:* The final in-gathering of the exiles is also associated with the blowing of the horn. Isaiah 27:13 says, "And it shall come to pass in that day, that the great trumpet shall be blown, and they shall come which were ready to perish in the land of Assyria, and the outcasts in the land of Egypt, and shall worship the Lord in the holy mount at Jerusalem."

» *Number 10:* The shofar relates to the resurrection. It is in this sense, according to Saadiah Gaon, the ancient Jewish rabbi, that Isaiah wrote in Isaiah 18:3: "All ye inhabitants of the world, and dwellers on the earth, see ye, when he lifteth up an ensign on the mountains; and when he bloweth a trumpet, hear ye."

According to the Talmud, Rabbi Johanan, who lived in the third century, wrote that on that day, some future Rosh Hashanah, three books will be opened before God. One is the Book of Life, in which the names of the just are entered and confirmed. One is the Book of Death, in which the wicked are entered, and the third is the book for those who are neither wholly just nor wholly wicked, in whose case the verdict is delayed until the Day of Atonement.

This picturesque description seems to concur with the New Testament concept of the Tribulation period. Those whose names are written in the Lamb's Book of Life, having been saved by the blood of the Lamb, be raised and raptured into Heaven. Those who have refused Christ as Savior will be doomed to judgment. However, there is a third group of people who will be given an opportunity to be saved during the days from Rosh Hashanah to Yom Kippur. Those seven Days of Awe represent the Tribulation period. From Revelation, we know that 144,000 Jews will be saved and a great multitude of people from every nation under the sun will be converted during the Tribulation period.

Quite a story is wrapped around the three Jewish festivals of the Feast of Trumpets, the Day of Atonement, and the Feast of Tabernacles. Rather strangely, the first four Jewish holy days were prophetically fulfilled on the very day of each feast. Will the prophecies of the last three come to pass on the day of each feast? Well, that is yet to be seen. But keep your ears open, for one of these days we're going to hear the sound of the great trumpet ... and we'll be gone.

Chapter 2

The Days of Affliction

Once the Tribulation period has begun and the Antichrist is revealed, any person who is knowledgeable concerning Bible prophecy will be able to determine the succession of events and accurately pinpoint both the Abomination of Desolation perpetrated by the Antichrist and the date for the glorious appearing of our Lord Jesus Christ.

The 144,000 Jews who are sealed by the Holy Spirit at the beginning of the Tribulation period will surely be knowledgeable enough to know the date for the coming of their Messiah, the Lord Jesus Christ. The reason we do not know today is that God's time schedule begins with the Tribulation, and we have not yet reached that point.

In Matthew 24:36, Jesus said: "But of that day and hour knoweth no man..." Four verses later He explained what event He was talking about. He said: "Then shall two be in the field; the one shall be taken, and the other left. Two women shall be grinding at the mill; the one shall be taken, and the other left. Watch therefore: for ye know not what hour your Lord doth come"(Matthew 24:40–42).

The Rapture of the church is the event that is shrouded in mystery. For men to say the Rapture will occur on a certain day, in a certain year, is unwise. It is obvious, however, that once the Tribulation period has begun, and the Antichrist is revealed, it will be possible to calculate the date for the Second Coming of Christ. But that privilege, if it be any comfort, will be left to the Jew, who must endure the Tribulation period. I am thankful that Christ has promised the believer an escape from the wrath of God by way of the Rapture.

It is possible that the Rapture of the church and the resurrection of the dead in Christ will occur on some future Rosh Hashanah, the Jewish New Year, for this is the Jewish holy day that foreshadows that great event. But the Jews were not even allowed to calculate Rosh Hashanah by a mathematical formula. The Jewish people were to watch each year for the coming of that day. On the last day of the month Elul, just prior to the beginning of the Jewish New Year, the Jewish people station themselves to watch for the new moon. This marked the beginning of Rosh Hashanah in the days of the Bible.

About the third or fourth century A.D., after the great Diaspora, when the Jews were scattered from their native land into all the countries of the world, the Jews began to calculate the date for Rosh Hashanah, in violation of God's Word.

Just as the ancient Jew would watch for the beginning of Rosh Hashanah, we are commanded by our Savior to watch for the Rapture of the church. When Rosh Hashanah was proclaimed, the ram's-horn trumpets were blown. Likewise, one day we shall hear the great heavenly trumpet, and the dead will be raised, and the church raptured.

There is something unusual, however, about the celebration of Rosh Hashanah. It is observed for two days instead of one. Perhaps prophetically it represents two events instead of one. We know it represents the blowing of the great shofar trumpet and the resurrection of the dead. But it may also represent the visible appearing, seven years later, of our Savior during the battle of Armageddon, when He comes in the clouds of glory with tens of thousands of His saints, for it is on Rosh Hashanah that the Jewish people proclaim God as King of the universe.

Following the celebration of Rosh Hashanah on the first and second days of the month of Tishri, there are seven days of penitence from the third day of Tishri until the ninth. These seven Days of Affliction for the Jewish people are a prophetic reference to the seven years of Tribulation. One day, in this case, equals one year.

This is not unusual, for there are other prophecies in the Old Testament where a day is made to equal a year. At Kadesh-Barnea God pronounced a judgment upon the people of Israel. Because of their unbelief, God proclaimed to Moses that the people would have to wander in the wilderness for forty years—a year for each day of the forty days the spies had spent in the Promised Land. Again, in Ezekiel 4:4–6, God commanded the prophet to lie on his left side for three hundred and ninety days, and then to lie on his right side for forty days to picture God's judgment upon Israel and Judah because of their unbelief. Here God told Ezekiel that His judgment would be upon the people for a total of four hundred and thirty years, a year for each day Ezekiel had lain on his side. So, it is not unusual for a single day to prophetically represent an entire year of God's judgment. These seven Days of Penitence, then, picture the seven years of the Tribulation.

During these seven Days of Penitence observed each year by the Jewish people, three days are prominent. They are called the Fast of Gedaliah, observed on the first day; Shabbat Shuvah, observed on the fourth day; and Erev Yom Kippur, observed on the seventh day.

Solomon's Temple

The Fast of Gedaliah is observed in remembrance of the murder of Gedaliah, son of Ahikam, during the days of the Babylonian occupation of Jerusalem. After the destruction of Solomon's Temple in 586 B.C., the king of Babylon nominated Gedaliah governor of the country. Ishmael, of the Judean royal family, came to Gedaliah at Mizpah and murdered him as they were partaking of a meal together. This murder was said to have taken place on Rosh Hashanah and is observed by the Jewish people each year on the day following Rosh Hashanah. In the book of Zechariah, the prophet Zechariah refers to the Fast of Gedaliah as the "fast of the seventh month" (7:5). In that chapter, a delegation of Jewish men came from Babylon to Jerusalem to inquire of the priests which were in the House of the Lord, saying, "... Should I weep in the fifth month, separating myself, as I have done these so many years?" (verse 3).

The fast of the fifth month was observed on the ninth day of the month of Av, the date on which the temple of Solomon was destroyed. Zechariah 7:4–5 says: "Then came the word of the Lord of hosts unto me, saying, Speak unto all the people of the land, and to the priests, saying, When ye fasted and mourned in the fifth and seventh month, even those seventy years, did ye at all fast unto me, even to me?"

The fast of the seventh month is still observed by the Jewish people today on the first day of the seven Days of Penitence, between Rosh Hashanah and Yom Kippur. The Sabbath day observed during this time is called Shabbat Shuvah. It is observed with the reading of the words, "Return, O Israel, unto the Lord thy God." Today, in most Jewish congregations, Shabbat Shuvah is also observed with a sermon from the rabbi, or minister of the synagogue. His message is expected to arouse the congregation to repentance and good deeds. Prophetically, this seems to correlate with the middle of the Tribulation period when the Antichrist commits the Abomination of Desolation spoken of by Daniel the prophet. It is also during the Tribulation period that "Mystery, Babylon the Great, that great city which reigneth over the kings of the earth" is destroyed by fire. In Revelation 18:4, a great voice proclaims from heaven, "Come out of her, my people, that ye be not partakers of her sins, and that ye receive not of her plagues." How fitting that in the middle of this seven Days of Penitence, the Jewish people read the Scripture, "Return, O Israel, unto the Lord thy God." The Fast of Gedaliah, observed on the first of these seven days, in memory of the murder of their beloved governor, could well represent the beginning of the Tribulation period and the battle of Gog and Magog, when Russia makes her Invasion against Israel.

Shabbat Shuvah, observed during these seven days, could well represent a worldwide exodus of Jews from all the countries of the world, particularly "Mystery Babylon," to their home country and their sacred city, Jerusalem.

The third special day observed during these seven Days of Awe is called Erev Yom Kippur, or "The Eve of Yom Kippur." It is observed on the seventh day and could well have a prophetic significance to the seventh year of the Tribulation period. This day preceding Yom Kippur is regarded as a semi-festival, which is usually spent in preparing for the Day of Atonement. Early in the morning, often before breakfast, the religious Jew takes a chicken and waves it above his head, while at the same time he recites this verse three times: "This is my substitute, this is my exchange, this is my atonement; this fowl will go to its death, and I shall enter a

The "Kapparot" Ceremony, "This is my substitute."

good and long life in peace." The ceremony is symbolic and reminiscent of the temple sacrifices.

One of the ideas behind the atonement sacrifice in the temple is that guilt is transferred to the sacrificial animal which pays the penalty for man's sin, while the person is cleansed. Through the offering of the animal, the person should be brought to the realization that it is he who should in reality be paying the penalty. After the brief ceremony, the chicken is redeemed with money which is given to the poor, and it is immediately slaughtered to be eaten for the meal preceding the Fast of Yom Kippur. The intestines of the chicken are thrown away in a place where the birds can eat them.

One day, in the battle of Armageddon, when it looks as if the Jewish people will have to pay the ultimate price for their unbelief, a spirit of repentance will come over them and they will turn to Jesus Christ as their Messiah axnd beg for forgiveness. They will have no choice. The genocide of the Jewish people will be imminent. Half of the city of Jerusalem will have fallen to the enemy, the houses rifled, and the women ravished. When the Jewish people are finally driven to repentance, a substitute sacrifice will be given. Instead of the Jewish people being destroyed, the armies of the world will be destroyed. Revelation 14:20 tells us that instead of the blood of Jews running in the streets, the blood of gentiles will flow up to the horses' bridles (approximately four and one-half feet) for the length of the land of Israel (two hundred miles).

Just as the birds are invited to eat the entrails of the chicken, Revelation 19:17–18 describes:

> ... an angel standing in the sun; and he cried with a loud voice, saying to all the fowls that fly in the midst of heaven, Come and gather yourselves together unto the supper of the great God; That ye may eat the flesh of captains, and the flesh of mighty men, and the flesh of horses, and of them that sit on them, and the flesh ofall men, both free and bond, both small and great.

It is also on Erev Yom Kippur that the Jewish people pray a confessional prayer of repentance before eating the sacrificed chicken. Another custom, seldom seen nowadays, is to receive lashes. At one time, lashes were a common form of punishment by the communal authorities. On Erev Yom Kippur, token blows, usually with a leather strap, are administered lightly. The penitent Jew recites the short confessional while the striker of the blows recites, "For He is merciful and forgives iniquity." How reminiscent of Isaiah 53:4–5! "Surely he hath borne our griefs, and carried our sorrows ... But he was wounded for our transgressions, he was bruised for our iniquities: the chastisement of our peace was upon him; and with his stripes we are healed."

How significant, too, that these things should be observed on the last day of the seven Days of Penitence, representing the seventh year of the Tribulation period. After the seven Days of Penitence comes Yom Kippur, the Day of Atonement. It is the most solemn day of the Jewish year and is the climax to the Days of Awe. Prophetically, it represents the conclusion of the seven years of Tribulation, when the Jewish people receive their Day of Atonement. It is the day on which both the Jew as an individual and the nation as a whole are cleansed of their sins and granted atonement.

The concept that a man can achieve atonement for his sins is basic to Judaism. Man is a dynamic organism who has free choice to do good or evil, But even after having committed evil, he can regain his former purity through atonement. Yom Kippur, as a day of atonement, concerns primarily the Jewish people AS A NATION rather than the atonement of the individual—the observance of Passover represents the atonement of the individual. In the ancient days of the temple in Jerusalem, the high priest acted as the representative of the people as a whole. A great part of the atonement service was for the nation as a whole. Even today, the confessional prayers are conducted in the plural form, thereby including all Israel.

Traditionally, Yom Kippur is the day on which Moses came down from Mount Sinai with the second two tablets of stone after obtaining God's forgiveness for Israel's sin with the golden calf. This day was set aside for generations to come as a day of forgiveness for the Jewish people. The ancient Jewish rabbis have written that during the Second Temple period, it was customary to tie some red wool to the temple gate which would turn white as a sign that the people had found forgiveness. It is also recorded by the ancient rabbis that during the forty years before the destruction of Herod's Temple in A.D. 70 that red wool tied to the temple gate remained red. The rabbis concluded that God was saying, "I will not forgive, I will not forgive."

Apart from the description of the Yom Kippur ceremony

in Leviticus 23:27–32, there is no information in the Bible as to how the day was observed prior to the Babylonian exile. There is a detailed description of the atonement service in the Second Temple period found in the Mishnah. Fragments of an order of prayer for the Day of Atonement have also been found in one of the caves at Qumran on the northwestern shore of the Dead Sea.

It is remarkable how little the content and theme of Yom Kippur has changed during these past two thousand years. There is a famous description by Rabbi Simeon Ben Gamaliel of Yom Kippur, in which he writes that the maidens of Jerusalem would go forth, all dressed in white, and would call out to the young men to choose each man a wife for himself. The plain girls would say, "Set not your eyes on beauty," and the beautiful girls would say, "Set not your eyes on family lineage." This may picture the bride of Christ, representing both the gentile believers of this dispensation and the Jewish believers of the Old Testament. One can almost hear the plain bride, or Jewish believers, saying to Christ, "Set not your eyes on beauty," and the beautiful bride, the New Testament church, saying, "Set not your eyes on family lineage."

In the final analysis, we learn from Revelation 21 that both the Jewish and gentile believers in Christ are members of the bride of Christ. When John was carried away in the spirit to a great and high mountain and was shown that great city, the holy Jerusalem, descending out of heaven from God, he described it as having twelve gates, whereon were written the names of the twelve tribes of Israel, and twelve foundations, wherein were written the names of the twelve apostles of the Lamb. The New Jerusalem, then, will be the eternal dwelling place of both the Jewish believers and the gentile believers in Christ.

Only in the Book of Jubilees do we find Yom Kippur connected with mourning. The day on which Jacob heard of Joseph's supposed death was the tenth of Tishri, and because of Jacob's grief, this day was ordained as a day for seeking atonement. The goat, offered in the temple as an atonement sacrifice, was a reminder of the goat which Joseph's brothers slaughtered. They dipped his coat in the goat's blood and sent it to Jacob to deceive him after selling Joseph. Joseph, by the way, was made governor of Egypt, second to Pharaoh, on Rosh Hashanah, the first day of Tishri. Rosh Hashanah also marked the beginning of the seven-year famine in Egypt. Joseph, as governor of the land, revealed himself to his brothers two years later. His revelation, as brother to the sons of Jacob, occurred somewhere in the month of Tishri. How prophetic! One day the Lord Jesus Christ, who was rejected by His brethren, and of whom Joseph was a type, will return to be declared King over a gentile world and be revealed to the Jewish people as the Messiah whom they rejected.

Chapter 3

The Day of Atonement

On Yom Kippur, the Day of Atonement, the book of Jonah is read in the synagogue. It has a prophetic significance. The story divides naturally into three parts. In the first part, Jonah tries to escape from his destiny, but he cannot. The second part demonstrates the efficacy of repentance, both when Jonah repents to do the will of God, and when Nineveh repents and is spared the judgment of God. The third section shows how God explains the workings of His providence to Jonah. God demonstrates to him His love for His creatures, whose lives are dear to

Jonah represents the Jewish people who have tried to escape from their destiny but cannot. God's judgment has thus been unleashed upon His people. Finally, Jonah repents—as will the 144,000 Jews of the Tribulation, who will carry out their message of judgment to the world. Finally, instead of utterly destroying the world, God redeems mankind by establishing the Millennial reign of Christ. Jonah, of course, also represents the Lord Jesus Christ, who took the punishment of Israel upon Himself as their substitute, and thus was in the heart of the earth for three days and three

The book of Jonah is read each year on Yom Kippur.

nights. Jesus referred to this in Matthew 12:40: "For as Jonas was three days and three nights in the whale's belly; so shall the Son of man be three days and three nights in the heart of the earth."

Yes, Jesus took Israel's punishment, and He took our punishment as well on the cross of Calvary. One day He will return to complete the work of redemption and fulfill the prophecies of Yom Kippur, the Day of Atonement.

The ritual of the ancient high priest on the Day of Atonement during the days of the temple period is most interesting. For seven days before Yom Kippur, the high priest lives in the temple precincts to prepare himself for the ritual sacrifice. There are two kinds of services on Yom Kippur: the regular everyday service, and the specific Yom Kippur service. For the regular temple service, the high priest wears his normal priestly garments ornamented with gold. But for the special Yom Kippur service he wears white, for the gold evokes the memory of the golden calf. Several times during the day the high priest must change his clothes from gold to white, and back again. Every time he does this, as well as at the beginning of the day's service, he sanctifies himself by a ritual immersion.

One of the principal parts of the special atonement service in the temple consists of prayers, recited by the high priest over the sacrifice animals. During these prayers the high priest speaks the holy name, the unutterable, ineffable name of God. Three times the high priest recites these atonement prayers, and in each of these prayers he pronounces the ineffable name of God three times.

The first prayer is recited when the high priest places his hands on the head of the bullock and prays for atonement for himself and his family. Later, he again uses the same bullock, and this time included in his prayer are the priests who were the descendants of Aaron. The third prayer requests atonement for the whole people.

For this prayer the scapegoat is used, called the Azazel goat. The order of atonement is not accidental, nor does it denote self-interest. Before the high priest could become the people's representative in their atonement, he first had to be utterly free from sin himself. Similarly, the priests who helped with the service had to have their sins atoned for before it was possible to seek atonement for the people as a whole. The scapegoat, or Azazel goat, was one of a pair. Two goats were used for this part of the service. One of the goats was to be used for a sacrifice, and his blood would be sprinkled upon the Mercy Seat of the Ark of the Covenant. The other goat would be taken out to the wilderness of Judea, near the area of Qumran, and driven over a cliff. When the high priest first received the two animals, he drew lots to decide which goat should be sacrificed as a sin offering for the Lord. On one lot was written the words, "A sin offering for the Lord," and on the other lot the words "For Azazel." As the high priest drew the lots, he would raise the hand in which he held the lot for the sin offering and cry aloud, "A sin offering for the Lord," again using the ineffable name of God.

The High Priest on Yom Kippur

It was considered a good omen if the lot for the sin offering came up in the high priest's right hand, for right is symbolic of good, and left is symbolic of evil. The ancient Jewish rabbis related that during the forty years prior to the destruction of the temple in A.D. 70, this lot always came up in the high priest's left hand. They wrote that it was one of the signs of the impending doom placed by God upon the Temple of Herod. The sacrificial goat was then slaughtered, and its blood sprinkled before the Ark of the Covenant in the Holy of Holies. Afterward, the second goat, or the scapegoat, was taken by the high priest, who rested his hands upon its head and recited the atonement prayer on behalf of all Israel. The goat, which then carried all of Israel's sins, was taken out to the Judean desert and pushed backward over a high cliff to its destruction.

Neither the Bible nor the Mishnah explains the inner meaning of this ceremony. However, we can see the prophetic significance of the two goats. They represent the Messiah in His two natures. The sacrifice goat represents the Lord Jesus Christ, who in His humanity was sacrificed for the sins of all men. Remember, it was John the Baptist who proclaimed one Rosh Hashanah day, "Behold the Lamb of God, which taketh away the sin of the world" (John 1:29). John made this proclamation just ten days before the high priest sacrificed the atonement animal in the Jerusalem temple. The scapegoat represented the Lord Jesus Christ, who in His deity carried our sins into the wilderness of God's forgetfulness. God placed our sins behind His back to remember them no more (Isaiah 38:17). This is seen also in the Toshlek ceremony, where the prophet Micah is quoted as saying, "... thou wilt cast all their sins into the depth of the sea" (Micah 7:19). Every time the high priest uttered the ineffable name of God, the people who were gathered in the court of the temple would fall on their faces and say, "Blessed be his glorious sovereign name forever and ever." That part of Yom Kippur is still practiced in the synagogues today.

On the ancient Day of Atonement, the high priest would enter the Holy of Holies three times—once with a special incense offering and twice to sprinkle the blood of the sacrifices. The people waiting in the courtyard of the temple were unable to see the high priest until he emerged from the outer sanctuary. It was believed that if the high priest was unworthy to enter the Holy of Holies, he would not survive. For this reason, a rope was tied to the leg of the high priest so that if he collapsed while in the presence of God, his body could be pulled from the inner sanctuary. As far as we know, history has never recorded the death of a high priest while in the Holy of Holies.

When the high priest entered the inner sanctuary with the blood of the sacrificed animal, he would sprinkle the blood upon the Mercy Seat, which represented the throne of God. After three hours in the darkness of the Holy of Holies, the high priest would emerge with the empty basin, hold it high, and proclaim, "It is finished." The people were then confident that the sacrifice had been accepted and their sins had been forgiven.

Prophetically, the blood atonement found its fulfillment on Calvary. Our High Priest, the Lord Jesus Christ, has taken His blood into the presence of God. The ultimate fulfillment will come to pass when our High Priest returns from the Holy of Holies of God's presence in Heaven to proclaim, "It is finished indeed."

At the close of the day following the afternoon service, as the sun reaches treetop height, the Neilah service is recited. This is the concluding service of the Day of Atonement. *Neilah* means "closing." The full name of the Neilah service is *Ne'ilat Ha Shearim,* "the closing of the gates." It refers to the daily closing of the temple gates at sunset, but prophetically represents the closing of the heavenly gates when all who are going to be saved will be saved, and the gate of Heaven will be shut.

At the close of the Neilah service, the shofar is blown on Yom Kippur, even if it is a sabbath, because it is already night. Various reasons are given for the blowing of the shofar. It is a reminder of the Jubilee year when all property is returned to its original owners, and all Jewish slaves are set free. This was announced by the blowing of the shofar on Yom Kippur. Again, the prophetic reference to the Second Coming of Jesus Christ is obvious. When Jesus returns amid the battle of Armageddon, He will establish His Jubilee, when all property throughout planet earth will be returned to its original owner, and every spiritual slave will be set free. Incidentally, the Jubilee is always announced by the blowing of the shofar on Yom Kippur in the forty-ninth year and the seventh month.

The blowing of the shofar trumpet at the end of Yom Kippur is also an allusion to Psalm 47:5: "God is gone up with a shout, the Lord with the sound of a trumpet." When God concluded the Sinai visitation and went up from the mount, the blast of the horn was heard, and it signified the termination of God's presence on the mountain.

In Jerusalem, it was customary to blow the shofar at the Western Wall. Following the Arab riots of 1929, the British mandatory authorities set up a committee of inquiry, followed by an international committee, which decided that, although the Jews had uncontested right to worship at the wall, they were not to blow the shofar there. The Jews regarded this ruling as a searing humiliation, and every year, nationalist youth would make it a point of honor to blow the shofar at the wall at the termination of

Yom Kippur, despite the danger from the Arabs and the intervention of the British police. Many of these youths were arrested and imprisoned.

Rabbi Shlomo Goren

Immediately following the capture of the old city of Jerusalem in 1967, Rabbi Shlomo Goren, who at that time was the chief chaplain of the Israel Defense Forces, blew the shofar at the Western Wall as a symbol of its redemption.

After the concluding service at the end of Yom Kippur, the Jewish people say to each other, "The next year, in Jerusalem." Only twice a year is this wish expressed — once at the termination of the Haggadah on Passover night, and once on Yom Kippur. This is in accordance with the difference of opinion between two ancient rabbis, Rabbi Elliazer and Rabbi Joshua, as to whether the Messiah will come to redeem Israel in Nisan or in Tishri.

In the Bible, Yom Kippur is described as *Shabbat Shabbaton,* "a sabbath of sabbaths." It is a sabbath, and all the commandments of the sabbath apply also to Yom Kippur, but it transcends the sabbath in sanctity because of the sacrificial service, and by virtue of its ultimate purpose. It also differs from the sabbath in the five forms of self-denial practiced on Yom Kippur as a part of the repentance ritual. These forms of self-denial, or afflictions, affecting the basic functions of the human body, make Yom Kippur even more a day of rest than the regular sabbath.

Yom Kippur is referred to four times in the Pentateuch—three times in Leviticus and once in Numbers. Leviticus 16 describes the sacrificial service on the Day of Atonement. Yom Kippur is mentioned again in the list of festivals, and a third time in connection with the Year of Jubilee. In the book of Numbers, the sacrifices of the day are listed. In each instance, except in the reference to the Jubilee year, the Bible stresses the commandment that a person must afflict himself. This commandment is directly related to the atonement which is granted on Yom Kippur. How prophetic that during the seven-year Tribulation period, the Jewish people will be afflicted more severely than any nationality of people in the history of humanity. The holocaust of Germany during the 1940s is not to be compared with the attempted genocide of the Jewish people during the war of Armageddon.

The affliction of Yom Kippur is observed by the Jewish people today through the method of fasting. Fasting appears frequently in the Bible as a sign of repentance. The people of Nineveh fasted after hearing Jonah's message. So did Esther and the Jews fast the three days before she risked her life by going uninvited to see King Ahasuerus. Fasting also, according to the Jewish religion, served the purpose of enhancing the spiritual inner man. By restraining the material requirements of the body, the mind can focus more clearly on the spiritual. A fast also reduces the fat content of the body, which is reckoned as if the worshiper had brought a sacrifice, the fat of which is offered on the altar of God. Washing and bathing is prohibited only when it causes gratification or comfort. For this reason, a Jewish person does not wash his hands or face on Yom Kippur. As the evening sun sets at the end of Yom Kippur, the fast is broken and it is considered commendable to eat and drink.

The high holy days, that of Rosh Hashanah and Yom Kippur, are remarkable for the impact they make on the Jewish people. The Days of Awe, those seven days between Rosh Hashanah and Yom Kippur, seem to embody the whole spirit of Judaism. Thus, for the religious Jew, they become the climax of the year, and prophetically they represent the climax of the centuries. It is surprising how little the high holy days have changed in the course of two thousand years. They have remained essentially the same since the days of the Second Temple, except for the sacrifice made on Yom Kippur, and the entrance of the high priest into the Holy of Holies, for the Jews have no temple today.

Originally, the Holy of Holies contained the Ark of the Covenant, with the tablets of stone and the Torah. In the Second Temple, the Holy of Holies remained completely empty, much to the astonishment of Pompey, the Roman general, who, in 63 B.C. forced his way into the inner sanctuary.

When the high priest entered the Holy of Holies on the Day of Atonement, he was completely alone. As the representative of the Jewish people, this was understood as a direct confrontation, once a year, of the people with God. Ancient Jewish rabbis claimed that even the angels were denied access to this encounter. Someday, on that future Day of Atonement, the Messiah will make His exit from the heavenly Holy of Holies. In Revelation 11:15,19, the Apostle John describes it this way:

> And the seventh angel sounded; and there were great voices in heaven, saying, The kingdoms of this world are become the kingdoms of our Lord, and of his Christ; and he shall reign for ever and ever. ... And the temple of God was opened in heaven, and there was seen in his temple the ark of his testament: and there were lightnings, and voices, and thunderings, and an earthquake, and great hail.

Yes, on that future Day of Atonement, the temple of God will be opened in Heaven and our High Priest will come forth at the sound of the seventh trumpet to judge the wicked and to establish His Kingdom.

Chapter 4

"Unto Us a Child Is Born"

We have studied the seven Jewish holy days found in Leviticus 23 and have considered their place in prophecy. The feasts of Passover, Unleavened Bread, and Firstfruits occur in the first month of the Jewish calendar, corresponding to our Easter in late March or early April, and prophetically find their fulfillment in the death, burial, and resurrection of Jesus Christ. Pentecost occurs fifty days after the Feast of Firstfruits and prophetically signifies the empowering of the Holy Spirit for the work of taking the gospel to every creature.

Beginning on the first day of the seventh month, there is yet another set of holy days. The Feast of Trumpets, or Rosh Hashanah, prophetically signifies the day when the trumpet shall sound, the dead shall be raised, and the living shall be changed. Ten days later, the Jews celebrate the Day of Atonement, or Yom Kippur. It prophetically signifies that day when Messiah shall come at the battle of Armageddon and make atonement for the sins of Israel. Five days later, on the fifteenth day of the seventh month, called Tishri on the Jewish calendar, the Feast of Tabernacles is celebrated.

Prophetically, it represents the Millennial reign of Christ. It is a magnificent picture of the future.

The prophetic significance of these seven Jewish holy days is astounding, to say the least. But there is yet another equally incredible parallel to be found in the time sequence of these seven Jewish holy days. In the seven Jewish feast days, there is a perfect picture of the gestation period in the development of a human child.

In the time sequence of the seven Jewish holy days, God gives us the beautiful story of the development of God's masterpiece—the creation of man. The story shows first that the Bible was written not by mere man, for thirty-five hundred years ago, man did not have a scientific understanding of gynecology or obstetrics. Quite the contrary, the Bible was written by One who possessed absolute knowledge of the meticulous birth process. More than that, it had to be written by the One who designed the birth process.

Second, these seven Jewish holy days prove divine creation. Through the magnificent parallels between the Jewish holy days and the development of the embryo, we learn that the theory of evolution is absolute nonsense.

After doing the research for our study on the high holy days, I came across a book by Zola Levitt entitled *The Seven Feasts of Israel.* Out of curiosity, I bought the book and read it to see if Mr. Levitt could add anything to the already detailed study I had just concluded. His prophetic treatment of the seven feasts of Israel coincided generally with what I had researched but was not as detailed as my own study. Feeling somewhat smug about the thoroughness of what I had considered an exhaustive study, I came to the second

Zola Levitt

chapter in this little book, entitled "Unto Us a Child Is Born." Here I found out, much to my chagrin, that I was still only a student of the Word, and not a scholar, for I still had much to learn. What I wish to share with you now is a profound study developed by Mr. Zola Levitt.

According to his story, he discovered the parallels between the seven Jewish holy days and the birth of a child quite by accident. He had been asked by his publisher to write a book on birth that could be used as a gift to be presented to Christian couples at the time of their blessed event. It was not intended to be a detailed book, because Mr. Levitt is not a doctor. He probably began his research with the idea of writing it from the viewpoint of the birth of our Savior. To get a better understanding of the birth process, he invited a physician, Dr. Margaret Mathison, to help him in his research. He asked her to tell him in some detail just how the baby is formed and how it grows.

Her first statement gave him a clue to the whole process. She said, "On the fourteenth day of the first month, the egg appears." That statement, "the fourteenth day of the first month," rang a bell. It is found in Leviticus 23:5: "In the fourteenth day of the first month ..." This statement is found in God's original instructions for the observance of Passover.

The Jews use an egg on the Passover table as a symbol of the new life they were granted by the sacrifice of the lamb in Egypt. The Christian world does not celebrate Passover as such. Instead, we celebrate Easter, but it corresponds with the same season of the year. Strangely enough, the symbol of Easter is an egg. Now, granted, the symbol of the egg at Easter comes from a pagan source, but it nevertheless corresponds beautifully with the Jewish symbol at Passover.

"On the fourteenth day of the first month the egg appears." Is it possible that God chose to correlate Passover with the birth process? If so, then the fertilization of the egg should coincide with the Feast of Unleavened Bread, which must occur the very next night: on the fifteenth day of the first month, according to Leviticus 23:6. So, Mr. Levitt asked the doctor how soon fertilization of the mother's egg must occur if pregnancy is to happen. Her answer was very clear and definite. "Fertilization must occur within twenty-four hours, or the egg will pass on." How incredible, and how perfect!

Now, the Feast of Unleavened Bread is a picture of the burial of Jesus Christ. Jesus said in John 12:24: "Verily, verily, I say unto you, Except a corn of wheat fall into the ground and die, it abideth alone: but if it die, it bringeth forth much fruit."

Again, Jesus referred to His body when He offered the unleavened bread on Passover night, in Matthew 26:26: "...Take, eat; this is my body."

Not only do these two momentous prenatal events (the

appearance of the egg and its fertilization) occur on the right days, but they are also the appropriate events to draw a parallel. The egg stands for Passover, and the idea of fertilization, the planting of the seed, for unleavened bread—the burial of our Lord. His crucifixion on Passover gave each of us the chance for everlasting life. His burial in the earth prepared for each of us the glorious resurrection to come.

The next question Mr. Levitt asked obviously concerned the Feast of Firstfruits. That feast does not occur in a perfectly timed cycle, as do the previous feasts of Passover and Unleavened Bread. The Feast of Firstfruits simply occurs on the Sunday during the week of Unleavened Bread. It could be the day after, or it could be almost a week later. Cautiously then, without revealing his motives, he asked the doctor what happened next in the birth process.

"Well," she said, "That's a little bit indeterminate. The fertilized egg travels down the tube at its own speed. It may take anywhere from two to six days before it implants." Two to six days—how incredible that it should be timed so perfectly with the Feast of Firstfruits. Then, too, she used the word "implants," which corresponds perfectly with the Festival of Firstfruits—the spring planting. This is also the correct medical term since "implantation" marks the moment when the fertilized egg arrives safely at its destination in the womb and begins its miraculous growth into a human being.

God designed these first three majestic feasts to correspond to the first steps in human conception. But will the system continue?

After Passover, Unleavened Bread, and Firstfruits, there is a long wait until Pentecost. Will there be some special event scheduled to occur within that time frame? Dr. Margaret Mathison put it this way: "Well, of course, we have a slowly developing embryo here for a long time. It goes through stages, but there is really no dramatic change until it becomes an actual fetus. That's the next big event." At that point, she showed Mr. Levitt a chart in the medical book picturing the first few weeks in the embryonic development.

Zola Levitt described it this way. He said, "I looked across the little pictures at what seemed like a little tadpole, which soon had flippers, and then began to look like a little man from Mars, and so on, down to the very last picture on the page. There I saw a human baby, and beside that drawing the very scriptural message, 'fifty days.'" Mr. Levitt, trying to conceal his excitement, asked the doctor, "Is the fiftieth day important?" "Well," she said, "Up until the fiftieth day you wouldn't know if you're going to have a duck or a cocker spaniel. But at the fiftieth day of the embryo, it becomes a human fetus."

No wonder the Psalmist wrote in Psalm 139:14–17:

> I will praise thee; for I am fearfully and wonderfully made ... My substance was not hid from thee, when I was made in secret, and curiously wrought in the lowest parts of the earth. Thine eyes did see my substance, yet being unperfect: and in thy book all my members were written, which in continuance were fashioned, when as yet there was none of them. How precious also are thy thoughts unto me, O God! how great is the sum of them!

Only God could design the embryonic growth of a human child and then build His holy feast days around its development. Likewise, the New Testament church was given life through the death, burial, and resurrection of the Savior, but took on the appearance of structured formation at Pentecost through the coming of the Holy Spirit. There are some who say that eternal life was imparted at Pentecost and that the New Testament church was born at Pentecost — just as there are those who say that a human fetus is not a human being until it reaches a certain stage of development, and thus can be aborted without facing the criminal consequences of committing murder. In my opinion, this study in the development of a human being, found in the timed sequence of God's seven feasts of Israel, answers the question most clearly. The church began at Calvary.

So far in our study, we have seen that life begins at conception, but that the embryo takes on the structured appearance of a human form around the fiftieth day. How perfectly and how beautifully this conforms to the miracle of Pentecost. From that point, progress in the growth of a baby is somewhat general, with nothing momentous happening until the first day of the seventh month. According to medical textbooks, at the first day of the seventh month, the baby's hearing is fully developed. The baby can then distinguish one sound from another. For example, a trumpet can be heard as a trumpet.

The next significant event in the development of the unborn child occurs ten days later, on the tenth day of the seventh month, and coincides perfectly with the Day of Atonement. Dr. Margaret

Mathison stated that the changes are in the blood. It is necessary for the fetal blood which carried the mother's oxygen through the baby's system to change in such a way that the baby can carry the oxygen that it will obtain upon birth. Technically, the hemoglobin of the blood must change from that of the fetus to that of a self-respirating and circulating human being. The fetus does not breathe, but rather depends on the oxygen obtained through the mother's blood circulation. Naturally, this system must be changed before birth and that change occurs, according to the textbook, in the second week of the seventh month, and to be precise, on the tenth day.

It is precisely on that day, according to the Mosaic law, that the high priest takes the blood into the Holy of Holies and presents it as an atonement for the sins of Israel. Leviticus puts it this way: "For the life of the flesh is in the blood: and I have given it to you upon the altar to make an atonement for your souls: for it is the blood that maketh an atonement for the soul" (Leviticus 17:11).

The "blood acceptable"—how fantastically it coordinates with the changing of the blood in the body of the unborn child to make it a "blood acceptable" because the life is in the blood. Just as the high priest enters the Holy of Holies with the blood of the sacrifice, the blood of the unborn baby enters the Holy of Holies of this earthly tabernacle. Remember, Paul said in 1 Corinthians 6: 19, "What? know ye not that your body is the temple of the Holy Ghost which is in you. ..."

How accurately the divine law of God coincides with His physical laws. All things in our universe are fashioned after the same pattern.

This again shows us that the divine plan of salvation was wrought by God. The necessity for a blood atonement is not the mere imagining of man. Man did not design deity. Deity designed man.

We have now reached the tenth day of the seventh month in the development of a human child. But the baby is not ready to be born. One more development is yet to occur, which coincides perfectly with the fifteenth day of the seventh month in the law of Moses, on which the Feast of Tabernacles is celebrated.

Dr. Margaret Mathison put it this way. "... that's when the lungs are developed, and as long as they get their little lungs going, we can bring them along, even if they are born at that early time. I'm afraid if they decide to come before those lungs are finished, then they have very little chance. But by the fifteenth day of the seventh month, a normal baby has two healthy lungs, and if born at that point, can take in its own air and live on it." What an incredible picture of the Feast of Tabernacles! The tabernacle is the house of the Spirit, just as the lungs are the tabernacle of the breath. God blew breath into Adam to make him become a living soul, and Christ breathed the Holy Spirit upon His disciples.

In Ezekiel 37, Ezekiel was taken in a vision to a valley filled with dry bones. There he saw the bones come together. He saw sinews and flesh come upon them. "And when I beheld, lo, the sinews and the flesh came up upon them, and the skin covered them above: but there was no breath in them" (Ezekiel 37:8). Note that the resurrected army had everything it takes to live except the breath. They had bones and flesh, feet and hands, eyes and ears, but as yet, there was no breath in them.

> Then said he unto me, Prophesy unto the wind, prophesy, son of man, and say to the wind, Thus saith the Lord God; Come from the four winds, O breath, and breathe upon these slain, that they may live. So I prophesied as he commanded me, and the breath came into them, and they lived, and stood up upon their feet, an exceeding great army.
>
> —Ezekiel 37:9–10

Now back to the baby. On the fifteenth day of the seventh month, the lungs are developed. From that day forward, the baby could be delivered and live. Everything is ready for birth. But wait a minute. That is only approximately two hundred days. What about the two hundred and eighty days it takes for the full gestation period in the birth of a human child? Remember, the Feast of Tabernacles is "the end of the road," the end of the feasts: the end of God's plan, and the beginning of the Kingdom. The baby would live if born at the Feast of Tabernacles, but there are another eighty days before the baby finally leaves its dwelling place of darkness and enters into the light—a total of two hundred and eighty days! Let us follow the system, then, to the two hundred and eightieth day of the Jewish calendar. Next, we come, right on schedule, to the Feast of Dedication. The Feast of Dedication, or Hanukkah, as it is called today, was not instituted by God on Mount Sinai. But it does, nevertheless, seem to have a divine origin.

According to Flavius Josephus, a Jewish historian who lived in the first century, Hanukkah was the result of a prophecy given by Daniel. According to Daniel 8:9–14, the Abomination of Desolation would result in the daily sacrifice at the temple being taken away. Then, after twenty-three hundred days, the sanctuary would be cleansed. This prophecy was fulfilled, according to Flavius Josephus, about one hundred and seventy years before Christ was born. It was then that Antiochus Epiphanes, a Syrian general, brought his army against the city of Jerusalem. He waged war for three and a half years and finally captured the Temple Mount. He desecrated the holy temple of God by sacrificing a sow upon the altar. Josephus said this was the Abomination of Desolation spoken of by Daniel the prophet.

The Jewish people continued to fight a guerrilla warfare against Antiochus Epiphanes and his Syrian soldiers, under the leadership of Judas Maccabeus. They were successful after three years of battle and set about to cleanse the sanctuary. When they entered the temple, they found only one precious can of consecrated oil, a day's supply, with which to maintain the eternal light in the great lampstand called the Menorah, also called the seven golden candlesticks. However, in those days the candle had not yet been invented. It was actually a series of seven oil lamps that rested upon a great pedestal. They poured the precious oil into the seven lamps and lit them to bring forth light. It would be eight days, however, before more oil could be supplied. During those eight days a miracle occurred. The one-day's oil supply lasted for eight days. So, in honor of the great light, the Jewish people added the Feast of Dedication to their calendar, celebrating the day when the temple was cleansed.

How perfect, then, is the picture, as the God of all creation cor-

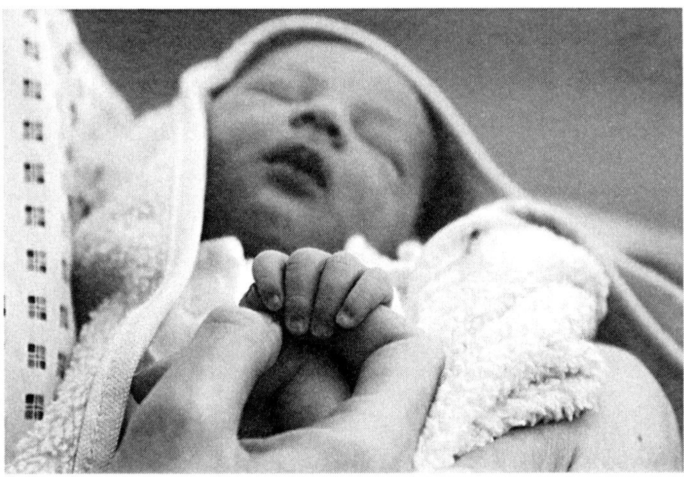

We wait expectantly for the birth. Maranatha!

related the feast days of the Jewish people with the development and birth of a human being.

One final note: The Millennial reign of Christ has been pictured in the Bible as being brought forth through a birth process. In Matthew 24, Jesus referred to the end-time signs of war, disease, famine, and earthquakes, as the travail of birth pangs. He said in verse 19: "And woe unto them that are with child ..." Then he said: "For then shall be great tribulation, such as was not since the beginning of the world to this time, no, nor ever shall be. And except those days should be shortened, there should no flesh be saved: but for the elect's sake those days shall be shortened" (Matthew 24:21–22).

Evidently Jesus is referring to the birth process concerning the birth of the golden age the Kingdom of Heaven when Christ shall reign as King of kings and Lord of lords. Just as the baby could be born any time after the two hundredth day, even so, the birth of our new age could occur without depending upon a precise schedule. No wonder Jesus said, "But of that day and hour knoweth no man ..." for indeed, the day cannot be calculated. We cannot know the exact day and hour of the birth of a child, but we can observe the travail of birth pangs. I am convinced we are near the delivery date. The Kingdom is about to be born.

A Final Word With You

May I urge you, dear Christian, to win as many people to Christ as you can while you can—for the time is short.

If you do not know our Lord Jesus Christ as your personal Lord and Savior, may I urge you to turn to Him right now.

Bow your head and pray a simple prayer. Repent of your sins and receive Jesus Christ as your personal Lord and Savior so that you might be saved from these great devastations which shall inevitably come upon an unbelieving human race.

Your prayer might go something like this:

Dear Lord, I know I am a sinner. Please forgive me for my sins. Come into my heart and life and save my soul. In Your holy name I pray. Amen.

ALSO AVAILABLE BY J.R. CHURCH

Guardians of the Grail

....and the men who plan to rule the world!

The Grail Legend takes you back through the centuries to view an emerging family dynasty who may soon attempt to establish One-World government.

J.R. Church reveals the story behind the developing United States of Europe. His research takes you back through the centuries to view an emerging family dynasty who may soon attempt to establish a one-world government. The framework for a global economy and political system is being set in place. Humanity is about to be deceived into accepting worldwide enslavement under the guise of "peace and prosperity." *Guardians of the Grail* tells of secret political combines, intrigues, and wars preparing mankind for the ANTICHRIST!

Order Your Copy Today!
1 (800) 652-1144
www.SWRC.com

More Faith-Building Books from Beacon Street Press

» ***Prayers of the Ancients*** by Kenneth C. Hill—How did people like Daniel, David, and Moses talk to God? What can we learn from their example? Your prayer life will be enriched as you study the greatest prayers in the Bible.

» ***By God's Grace: A Cancer Survivor's Testimony*** by Vaughn Shatzer—This life-changing story is an encouragement to everyone. Learn how the fiery trial of cancer brought the Shatzer family to a new level of trust, faith, patience, and hope in God.

» ***Jewish Roots of Christianity*** by Larry Stamm—In this biblical survey, Larry Stamm, a first-generation Holocaust survivor and Jewish follower of Jesus, examines the religion of the Old Testament and its ultimate fulfillment in Jesus Christ.

» ***The Shepherd*** by James Collins—In *The Shepherd,* James Collins teaches the 23rd Psalm verse-by-verse, explaining its extraordinary power to change lives. This book will help you rediscover the joy, inspiration, and peace of this beloved psalm.

» ***Panorama of Creation*** by Carl Baugh—Mankind's greatest battle, creation vs. evolution, is before us. Dr. Baugh scientifically proves that special creation is the only explanation for man's existence on this planet. Bonus chapter on dinosaurs.

» ***The Power of the Cross*** by Robert Lindsted—In *The Power of the Cross,* Dr. Lindsted teaches through the trial, crucifixion, and resurrection of Jesus Christ. Discover the significance of the seven sayings from the cross.

» ***Living in Today's World*** by Greg Patten – Greg shares timeless tales filled with compassion and love that are guaranteed to minister to multiple generations. Have your soul encouraged with these uplifting stories of *Living in Today's World.*

1 (800) 652-1144
www.SWRC.com

Order These Books from Beacon Street Press

» ***Digging Deeper*** by Larry Spargimino—In this volume, Dr. Spargimino answers relevant questions that every Christian has asked at one time or another. You will get the questions, the answers, and the scriptural reasons for the answers.

» ***Will the Church Go Through the Tribulation?*** by various—In this book, several authors consider separate but relative sections of both the Old and New Testaments, to see if the church will go through the Tribulation.

» ***Daniel the Prophet*** by Noah Hutchings—Dr. Hutchings teaches the book of Daniel, chapter by chapter and verse by verse. He reveals the prophecies concerning the end of the age that were meant for the final generation.

» ***The 12*** by James Collins—In *The 12,* James Collins explores the life and times of the Minor Prophets, revealing how these men who lived thousands of years ago have messages that are relevant and contemporary.

» ***Satan's 10 Most Believable Lies*** by Dave Breese—Dr. Breese describes ten of the enemy's false doctrines. Each chapter defines the lie and tells how to avoid the lie by using the truth found in Scripture.

» ***Petra in History and Prophecy*** by Noah Hutchings—You will be amazed at the most fascinating ghost town in the world, the city of Petra. Dr. Hutchings reveals how this area in southern Jordan will one day be Israel's hiding place.

» ***The Great Pyramid: Prophecy in Stone*** by Noah Hutchings—With words and pictures, Dr. Hutchings takes his readers on an exciting journey to tour the Great Pyramid of Cheops. Learn about its true past as the Pillar of Enoch!